Foundation
Teacher's Guide

Series editors: **Lindsay Pickton and Christine Chen**
Author: **Alison Milford**

HarperCollins
PUBLISHERS
200

William Collins' dream of knowledge for all began with the publication of his first book in 1819.

A self-educated mill worker, he not only enriched millions of lives, but also founded a flourishing publishing house. Today, staying true to this spirit, Collins books are packed with inspiration, innovation and practical expertise. They place you at the centre of a world of possibility and give you exactly what you need to explore it.

Collins. Freedom to teach.

An imprint of HarperCollins*Publishers*
The News Building
1 London Bridge Street
London
SE1 9GF

© HarperCollins*Publishers* Limited 2017

Browse the complete Collins catalogue at
www.collins.co.uk

10 9 8 7 6 5 4 3 2 1

ISBN 978-0-00-821549-1

Alison Milford asserts her moral right to be identified as the author of this work.

British Library Cataloguing in Publication Data

A catalogue record for this publication is available from the British Library.

Commissioned by Fiona McGlade

Series editors Lindsay Pickton and Christine Chen

Project managed by Natasha Paul

Developed by Hannah Hirst-Dunton

Edited by Frances Amrani

Proofread by Catherine Dakin

Cover design by Amparo Barrera

Cover artwork by Yello Studio Limited

Typesetting by 2hoots Publishing Services

Illustrations by Advocate Art

Production by Lauren Crisp

Printed and bound by CPI Group (UK) Ltd, Croydon, CR0 4YY

Photo acknowledgements
The publishers wish to thank the following for permission to reproduce photographs. Every effort has been made to trace copyright holders and to obtain their permission for the use of copyright materials. The publishers will gladly receive any information enabling them to rectify any error or omission at the first opportunity.

(t = top, c = centre, b = bottom, r = right, l = left)

P168 t Tom Gowanlock/Shutterstock, p168 cl Laura Dinraths/Shutterstock, p168 cc PsychoShadow/Shutterstock, p168 cr davemhuntphotography/Shutterstock, p168 bl Samuel Kornstein/Shutterstock, p168 br David Havel/Shutterstock, p169 Olly Molly/Shutterstock.

Contents

Treasure House Foundation Introduction

Welcome to Treasure House Teacher's Guide for Foundation

Welcome to the Treasure House Teacher's Guide. This guide provides a framework for an educational, creative and engaging literacy programme with a story-telling focus for EYFS planning and teaching throughout the Reception year. The guide contains 18 story-led or poem-led teaching sequences which focus on two main learning and development areas outlined in the 'Statutory Framework for the early years foundation stage' (EYFS).

These are:

Prime area

Communication and language

- Listening and attention

- Understanding

- Speaking

Specific area

Literacy

- Reading

- Writing

The sequences also contain a progression of phonics activities based on Phase 2 and 3 of the 'Letters and Sounds' phonics scheme. However, the activities and objectives are flexible enough to be used with other phonics schemes that you may be using in your planning.

Communication skills and development, letter and word recognition, early reading and writing skills, and the development of phonic knowledge are integral throughout all the sequences, as this is fundamental to the development of all literacy learning.

Each Treasure House Foundation sequence is a two-week story-led or poem-led topic which effectively interweaves the main literacy areas of communication, reading, writing and phonics into interesting and fun activities for the children. This enables them to become focused and engaged with their learning and develop an on-going interest and love in books, stories and poems.

A major part of Treasure House Foundation is its story-telling element. Each sequence offers guidance and suggestions on how to effectively read a story or perform a poem to the children so that they connect with its message, words, images or rhythms. A storytelling resource is also available on Connect, which allows you to show a storyteller performing the stories and poems.

We believe it is important that the children also have the opportunity to explore each story or poem further through play or other non-literacy activities. With that in mind, we have also created other child-led or adult-led activities and play experiences that involve other learning and development areas such as:

- Physical development

- Personal, social and emotional development

- Mathematics

- Understanding the world

- Expressive arts and design,

Treasure House Foundation is organised onto three story-led or poem/rhyme-led sequences for each half term and can be used as the basis of your literacy planning, potentially providing weeks of teaching inspiration. The selected picture book stories are a mix of well-loved titles and new exciting titles. We have also selected poems and rhymes which encourage participation and discussion.

These sequences can be adaptable to the needs of different classes or groups according to your professional judgment. The half term topic sequences can be used in any order and the activities can be adjusted to meet the needs of your class, and to fit with your broader teaching scheme. Their flexibility allows you to draw from your own experiences, and apply your own imagination, as frequently as you wish. This is a handbook that seeks to support and enhance teachers', as well as children's, skills and creativity.

About Treasure House Foundation

Treasure House is a comprehensive and flexible bank of print and digital resources covering the 2014 'Statutory framework for the early years foundation stage'.

Treasure House Foundation comprises:

- Print Teacher's Guide
- Print Workbook
- Online digital resources hosted on Collins Connect.

Treasure House Foundation Teacher's Guide

The Teacher's Guide contains 18 literacy sequences based around top-class stories and poems/rhymes. These are spread over the three school terms with one topic per half term. Each half term has three sequences linked to one main topic, with each title focusing on a sub-topic, for example Topic – Animals: Sub-topics: Birds, Bees, Sea creatures. We have suggested that each sequence would be effective carried out over a two-week period but this can be adapted to fit in with your own class planning and timetable.

The sequence topics are as follows:

Sequence overview chart

Term topics and sequence numbers	Anthology texts	Approximate duration
Term 1 (Autumn)		
1st half term topic: Ourselves		
1. My Body: poem	'*All About Me*' by Georgie Adams	2 weeks
2. What I Can Do: poem	'*Show and Tell*' by James Carter	2 weeks
3. Family and Friendship: story	'*Mog and Bunny*' by Judith Kerr	2 weeks
2nd half term topic: Colours		
4. Colours Around Us: poem	'*Painting*' by Irene Rawnsley	2 weeks
5. Rainbows: story	'*Elmer and the Rainbow*' by David McKee	2 weeks
6. Festival Colours: story	'*A Story of Diwali: The Festival of Light*' by Pippa Howard	2 weeks
Term 2 (Spring)		
1st half term topic: Food		
7. Apples: poem	'*The Apple*' by Gillian Floyd	2 weeks
8. Growing Food: traditional tale	'*The Enormous Potato*' by Aubrey Davis	2 weeks
9. Growing Plants: song rhyme/poem	'*Juba's Bean*' by Alison Milford	2 weeks
2nd half term topic: Animals		
10. Birds: traditional tale	'*Henny Penny*' by Vivian French and Sophie Windham	2 weeks
11. Bees: poem	'*Watching a Bumble-Bee*' by Wes Magee	2 weeks
12. Sea Creatures: rhyming story	'*Sharing a Shell*' by Julia Donaldson	2 weeks
Term 3 (Summer)		
1st half term topic: In The Air		
13. Kites: story	'*Blown Away*' by Rob Biddulph	2 weeks
14. Magical Flying!: story	'*The Magic Bed*' by John Burningham	2 weeks
15. Space and Stars: story	'*How to Catch a Star*' by Oliver Jeffers	2 weeks
2nd half term topic: Our World		
16. Fairs and Carnivals: poem	'*The Big Steel Band*' by Wes Magee	2 weeks
17. A Tale from Another Country: story	'*Mama Panya's Pancakes*' by Mary and Rich Chamberlin	2 weeks
18. Holiday Experiences: poem	'*Holiday Memories*' by June Crebbin	2 weeks

Sequence structure

Each sequence has four sections and is organised in the same way:

1. **Exploring the Story or Poem**
   - **Phase 1**: **Introduction to the story or poem**: Introducing the story/poem theme, what do the children know, sharing experiences, reading or performance of the text, questions and discussion about the story or poem and a related consolidation activity.
   - **Phase 2: Getting to know the story or poem**: Revisiting the text in more detail including activities linked to the story or poem's structure, vocabulary and message. This also includes a phonics activity.
   - **Phase 3: Exploring the story through role-play/ Performing the poem**: Activities using role-play, movement and performance.

2. **Literacy Activities**
   - A range of reading, writing and phonics activities related to the story or poem (a mix of games, interactive and group activities).

3. **Cross-curricular Activities**
   - A mix of fun, engaging adult-led and child-led activities and play suggestions linked to the story or poem that covers other EYFS Learning and Development areas such as Mathematics and Expressive Arts

4. **Sequence assessment**
   - A range of related assessment questions linked to the Learning Outcomes to help with observational assessment and end of sequence assessment.

Using a Treasure House Foundation teaching sequence

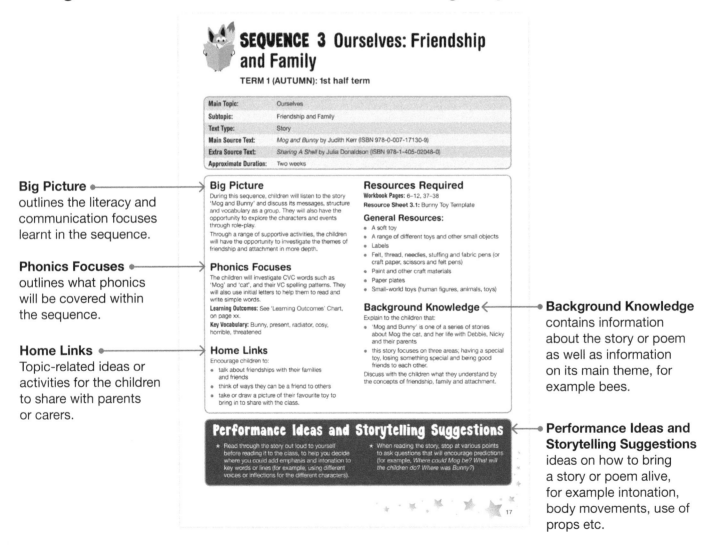

Big Picture outlines the literacy and communication focuses learnt in the sequence.

Phonics Focuses outlines what phonics will be covered within the sequence.

Home Links Topic-related ideas or activities for the children to share with parents or carers.

Background Knowledge contains information about the story or poem as well as information on its main theme, for example bees.

Performance Ideas and Storytelling Suggestions ideas on how to bring a story or poem alive, for example intonation, body movements, use of props etc.

Treasure House sequence structure

Each sequence has a reference table outlining the sequence structure. These show the plan for a two-week period but it can be adapted to suit your own planning and class or group timings.

Activity name

Approximation of activity time

A Literacy Activity
Literacy activity names

A Cross-curricular Activity
story or poem-linked other learning and development activities and play experiences.

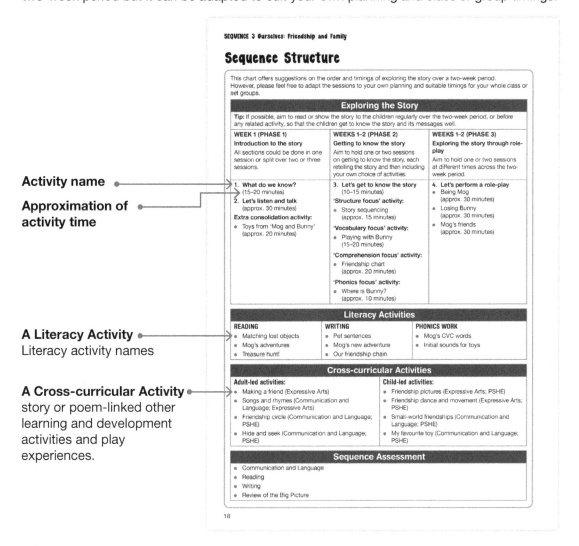

Sequence activities

Each activity is written in concise bulleted points with icons to suggest size of groups and whether they are adult-led or child-led.

These are:

 Adult-led with class/groups

 Adult-initiated with class/groups

 Groups

 Pairs

Individuals

Treasure House Workbook

This children's workbook focuses on developing and consolidating early phonological skills such as linking sounds to letters, recognising initial-letter sounds, blending and sounding out CVC, CVCC and CCVC words, looking at consonant digraphs and vowel graphemes and recognising tricky words. The content is linked to 'Letters and Sounds – Phase 2 and 3' but can also be used for most phonics programmes.

Treasure House on Collins Connect

Digital pupil resources for Treasure House are available on Collins Connect, an innovative learning platform designed to support teachers and pupils by providing a wealth of interactive activities.

Treasure House Foundation is organised into sequences, with each sequence containing:

- Editable Word, and PDF, versions of the sequence from the Teacher's Guide
- A bank of varied and engaging interactive activities, so children can practise their knowledge and skills
- Audio support to help children access the texts and activities
- Video of storyteller reading the main text
- In sequences where the main text is a poem, there is also an illustrated version of the poem and a version of the poem with storytelling cues.

EYFS framework links

The 'Statutory framework for the early years foundation stage, 2014' is organised into seven early learning goals. Of those seven, three are considered Prime areas:

- Communication and language
- Physical development
- Personal, social and emotional development.

The other five early learning goals are 'Specific areas', of which 'Literacy – reading and writing' is one of them.

With its creative, story and poem-led framework, Treasure House Foundation is dedicated to creating learning opportunities and experiences linked to the early learning goals for Communication and Language and Literacy.

Communication and Language

This is a prime early learning goal that encompasses Listening and Attention, Understanding, and Speaking. The main scaffolding throughout Treasure House Foundation is to offer the opportunity to children to experience wonderful, colourful and creative stories and poems in order to develop their communication skills through listening, speaking and answering simple questions about the texts, events, characters and ideas. They also have the opportunity to use role-play and performance to explore the stories and poems further. At the end of each sequence the children are encouraged to share their knowledge, experiences and achievements with their peers and teachers.

Literacy – Reading

Literacy is a Specific early learning goal which includes Reading and Writing. The Learning Outcomes for 30–50 month and 40–60+ month children include a further understanding of stories and their structure, the recognition of rhyme and rhythmic structures and the development in reading skills such as initial sounds and reading simple sentences. Fun and topic-related reading activities within each of the Treasure House sequences allow the children to focus on these different reading outcomes with the result that all the Learning Outcomes are covered by the end of the school year.

Literacy – Writing

The Learning Outcomes for Writing for 30-50 months and 40-60+ month children focus on their phonological development and knowledge in order to recognise initial-letter sounds and develop skills in blending and spelling simple words as well as names and simple sentences. The Treasure House sequences offer a range of writing activities that include writing sentences and their names, creating books, labels and working on phonological games and activities.

Learning through play

The Statutory framework for the early years foundation stage, 2014 states that the three ways of effective teaching and learning within the EYFS is through:

- Playing and exploring
- Active learning
- Creating and thinking critically.

Treasure House Foundation has embraced this by including a mix of adult-led and child-led play experiences and activities that allows the children to explore the stories and poems in their own time and through different methods. These can include small play, messy play, sand play, fancy dress and home corner, crafts, cooking, experiments, outdoor and indoor games, music, movement, show and tell and looking at displays, images and books related to the story theme.

Assessment in Treasure House Foundation

Assessment of a child's abilities and needs is essential during the Early Years Foundation Stage in order to gauge their progress as well as to enable teachers and teaching practioners to plan further activities and support if needed.

The most effective form of assessment for children in the EYFS is an on-going formative assessment using observational techniques, which is encouraged throughout the sequences in Treasure House Foundation. As the children take part in the various activities of a sequence, take note of what they say and do, how they interact with adults and their peers, and how they include the stories or poems in their vocabulary or play. Note their progress and highlight any support needed.

Observational assessment may be pre-planned with notes taken down of the child's responses and abilities within an activity or it can be totally spontaneous, when an unexpected important learning moment occurs.

Treasure House Foundation has created a Child observation sheet (page x) which you can use while the children take part in the different range of literacy activities within each sequence. It includes the Learning Outcome of an activity, the activity description, observation notes, assessment achievements and suggestions for further support or needs.

Keep the sheets together as a record of a child's progress of their Communication and Language and Literacy skills across the Reception Year, as you use the different topic-related sequences.

We have also produced a Learning Outcome chart (page xi) that focuses on Communication and language and the Literacy early learning goals so that you can see what learning outcomes are covered within each sequence enabling you to assess the child's level of development against each one.

Review of a sequence

At the end of each sequence there is a section called 'Review of the Big Picture'. Use this 'show and tell' style activity to find out what the children have learnt and enjoyed about the story or poem and its activities. Encourage each child to share their achievements and take note on what parts of the Big Picture objectives they have successfully covered, as well as areas for support.

Child observation sheet

Term: **Date:**

Child's name: **Age:**	**Topic:** **Sub-topic:**

Learning focus:
(listening, speaking, reading, writing, phonics)

Learning outcomes:
Communication and Language:

Literacy (reading, writing, phonics):

Activity name and description:
Adult-led/child-led   class / group / pair / individual

Observation notes:

Assessment:
Learning outcomes achieved:

Further support or needs:

Learning Outcomes Chart

Communication and language		Sequence																	
		1	2	3	4	5	6	7	8	9	10	11	12	13	14	15	16	17	18
Listening																			
30 to 50 months																			
Listen to others one to one or in small groups, when conversation interests them.		x	x	x	x	x	x	x	x	x	x	x	x	x	x	x	x	x	x
Listens to stories with increasing attention and recall.				x		x	x	x	x	x	x	x	x	x	x	x		x	
Joins in with repeated refrains and anticipates key events and phrases in rhymes and stories.		x		x	x	x	x	x	x	x	x	x	x	x	x	x	x	x	x
Focusing attention – still listen or do, but can shift own attention.		x	x	x	x	x	x	x	x	x	x	x	x	x	x	x	x	x	x
Is able to follow directions (if not intently focused on own choice of activity).		x	x	x	x	x	x	x	x	x	x	x	x	x	x	x	x	x	x
40 to 60+ months																			
Maintains attention, concentrates and sits quietly during appropriate activity.		x	x	x	x	x	x	x	x	x	x	x	x	x	x	x	x	x	x
Two-channelled attention – can listen and do for short span.		x	x	x	x	x	x	x	x	x	x	x	x	x	x	x	x	x	x
Make inferences on the basis of what is being said and done.																			
Understanding																			
30 to 50 months																			
Beginning to understand 'why' and 'how' questions.		x	x	x	x	x	x	x	x	x	x	x	x	x	x	x	x	x	x
40 to 60+ months																			
Responds to instructions involving a two-part sequence.		x	x	x	x	x	x	x	x	x	x	x	x	x	x	x	x	x	x
Understand humour, e.g. nonsense rhymes, jokes.									x	x							x		x
Able to follow a story without pictures or props.				x					x			x	x				x		x
Listens and responds to ideas expressed by others in conversation or discussion.		x	x	x	x	x	x	x	x	x	x	x	x	x	x	x	x	x	x

Communication and language

Communication and language	Sequence																	
	1	2	3	4	5	6	7	8	9	10	11	12	13	14	15	16	17	18
Speaking																		
30 to 50 months																		
Beginning to use more complex sentence to link thoughts (e.g. using and, because).					×					×		×	×	×	×		×	
Can retell a simple past event in correct order (e.g. went down slide, hurt finger).			×		×	×		×	×	×		×	×	×	×		×	
Uses talk to connect ideas, explain what is happening and anticipate what might happen next, recall and relive past experiences.	×	×	×	×	×	×	×	×	×	×	×	×	×	×	×	×	×	×
Questions why things happen and gives explanations. Asks e.g. who, what, when, how.	×	×	×	×	×	×	×	×	×	×	×	×	×	×	×	×	×	×
Uses a range of tenses (e.g. play, playing, will play, played).		×				×		×		×		×			×			×
Uses intonation, rhythm and phrasing to make the meaning clear to others.	×	×		×			×	×	×	×	×	×				×	×	×
Uses vocabulary focused on objects and people that are of particular importance to them.	×	×	×	×			×				×		×			×		×
Builds up vocabulary that reflects the breadth of their experiences.	×	×	×	×	×	×	×	×	×	×	×	×		×		×	×	×
Uses talk in pretending that objects stand for something else in play, e.g. 'This box is my castle.'					×		×	×	×	×		×	×	×	×	×	×	×
40 to 60+ months																		
Extends vocabulary, especially by grouping and naming, exploring the meaning and sounds of new words.	×	×	×	×	×	×	×	×	×	×	×	×	×	×	×	×	×	×
Uses language to imagine and recreate roles and experiences in play situations.	×		×	×	×	×	×	×	×	×	×	×	×	×	×	×	×	×
Links statements and sticks to a main theme or intention.	×	×	×	×	×	×	×	×	×	×	×	×	×	×	×	×	×	×
Uses talk to organise, sequence and clarify thinking, ideas, feelings and events.	×	×	×	×	×	×	×	×	×	×	×	×	×	×	×	×	×	×
Introduces a storyline or narrative into their play.			×		×	×	×	×	×	×	×	×	×	×	×	×	×	

Literacy

Reading

	Sequence																	
	1	2	3	4	5	6	7	8	9	10	11	12	13	14	15	16	17	18
30 to 50 months																		
Enjoys rhyming and rhythmic activities.	x	x		x			x			x	x	x				x		x
Shows awareness of rhyme and alliteration.	x	x		x			x		x	x	x	x				x		x
Recognises rhythm, in spoken words.	x	x		x			x	x	x	x	x	x				x		x
Listens to and joins in with stories and poems, one-to-one and also small groups.	x	x	x	x	x	x	x	x	x	x	x	x	x	x	x	x	x	x
Joins in with repeated refrains and anticipates key events and phrases in rhymes and stories.	x	x	x	x	x	x	x	x	x	x	x	x	x	x	x	x	x	x
Beginning to be aware of the way stories are structured.			x		x	x		x		x		x	x	x	x		x	
Suggest how the story might end.			x		x	x		x	x	x	x	x	x	x	x		x	
Listens to stories with increasing attention and recall.	x	x	x	x	x	x	x	x	x	x	x	x	x	x	x	x	x	x
Describes main story settings, events and principal characters.			x	x	x	x		x		x		x	x	x	x		x	
Shows interest in illustrations and print in books and print in the environment.	x	x	x	x	x	x	x	x	x	x	x	x	x	x	x	x	x	
Recognises familiar words and signs such as own name and advertising logos.	x	x		x		x	x							x		x		
Looks at books independently.					x				x								x	
40 to 60+ months																		
Continues a rhyming string.	x	x	x	x	x	x	x	x	x	x	x	x	x		x	x		x
Hears and says the initial sound in words	x	x	x	x	x	x				x	x	x	x	x	x	x	x	x
Can segment the sounds in simple words and blend them together and knows which letters represent some of them.	x	x	x	x	x	x	x	x	x	x	x	x	x	x	x	x	x	x
Links sounds to letters, naming and sounding the letters of the alphabet.	x	x	x	x	x	x	x	x	x	x	x	x	x			x	x	x
Begins to read words and simple sentences.	x	x	x	x	x	x	x	x	x	x	x	x	x	x	x	x	x	x
Uses vocabulary and forms of speech that are increasingly influenced by their experiences of books.		x	x		x	x	x	x	x	x		x		x	x	x	x	x
Enjoys an increasing range of books.			x		x			x	x	x		x			x	x	x	

Learning Outcomes Chart

Literacy

Writing — 40 to 60+ months	1	2	3	4	5	6	7	8	9	10	11	12	13	14	15	16	17	18
Gives meaning to marks they make as they draw, write and paint.	X	X	X	X	X	X	X	X	X	X	X	X	X	X	X	X	X	X
Begins to break the flow of speech into words.	X	X	X	X	X	X	X	X	X	X	X	X	X	X	X	X	X	X
Continues a rhyming slang.	X	X		X			X	X			X	X						X
Hears and says the initial sound in words.	X	X	X	X	X	X				X	X	X	X	X	X	X	X	X
Can segment the sounds in simple words and blend them together.	X	X	X	X	X	X	X	X		X	X	X	X	X	X	X	X	X
Links sounds to letters, naming and sounding the letters of the alphabet.	X	X	X	X	X	X	X			X	X	X	X	X	X	X	X	X
Uses some clearly identifiable letters to communicate meaning, representing some sounds correctly and in sequence.	X	X	X	X	X	X	X	X	X	X	X	X	X	X	X	X	X	X
Writes own name and other things such as labels, captions.	X	X	X	X	X	X	X	X	X		X	X			X			X
Attempts to write short sentences in meaningful contexts.	X	X	X	X	X	X	X	X	X	X	X	X	X	X	X	X	X	X

Phonics coverage chart

Phonics	1	2	3	4	5	6	7	8	9	10	11	12	13	14	15	16	17	18
s a t p	X	X	X	X	X	X	X	X	X	X	X	X	X	X	X	X	X	X
l n m d	X	X	X	X	X	X	X	X	X	X	X	X	X	X	X	X	X	X
g o c k	X	X	X	X	X	X	X	X	X	X	X	X	X	X	X	X	X	X
ck e w r	X	X	X	X	X	X	X	X	X	X	X	X	X	X	X	X	X	X
h b	X	X	X	X	X	X	X	X	X	X	X	X	X	X	X	X	X	X
f (ff) l (ll) ss	X	X	X	X	X	X	X	X										
j v w x y z(zz) qu								X		X	X							
ch sh th ng										X	X	X	X	X				
ai igh ar									X						X			
ee oo oa							X							X		X		
or ur ow								X							X			X
oi ear air																	X	X
ure er																X	X	
Tricky words						X						X		X			X	
Syllables	X				X	X										X		

SEQUENCE 1 Ourselves: My Body

TERM 1 (AUTUMN): 1st half term

Main Topic:	Ourselves
Subtopic:	My Body
Text Type:	Poem
Main Source Text:	'All About Me' by Georgie Adams, from *Time For a Rhyme* edited by Fiona Waters (ISBN 978-1-858-81695-1)
Extra Source Text:	*Zoom!* by Grace Nicholls (ISBN 978-0-006-64621-1)
Approximate Duration:	Two weeks

Big Picture

During this sequence, children will listen to the poem 'All about Me' and discuss its meaning, structure and vocabulary as a group. They will join in with the poem using actions, and will enact it.

The children will become familiar with action words and rhyming words and, through a range of supportive activities, will have the opportunity to find out more about their bodies and who cares for them by using songs, art, craft and games.

Phonics Focuses

The children will investigate words with one- and two-syllable beats, CVC spelling patterns and how they can use initial letters to help decode words.

Learning Outcomes: See 'Learning Outcomes' Chart, on pages xi–xiv.

Key Vocabulary: head, eyes, ears, nose, mouth, arms, elbows, knees, legs, feet, boring, squeezing, beat

Home Links

Encourage children to:

- think about how they use their bodies at home (for example, when eating, washing, hugging and sleeping)
- think about all the active things they like doing (for example, at the park)
- bring in something for 'show and tell' that demonstrates them using a part of their body.

Resources Required

Workbook Pages: 4–10

Resource Sheets 1.1–1.2: Body Parts; Split-pin Puppet

General Resources:

- Craft paper
- A small drum
- Craft materials (e.g. paints, pipe cleaners, straws, tape, sand, glue, fabric, glitter)
- Split pins
- Sports play equipment (e.g. bean bags, soft climbing blocks, pop-up tunnels)
- Paper plates

Background Knowledge

Explain to the children that:

- the poem 'All About Me' discusses different parts of the body and ways we can use them
- it is an active poem with action words that the children can copy and perform.

This activity is intended to allow them to explore and celebrate their own bodies, appreciating what they can do and how important it is to look after them.

Performance Ideas and Storytelling Suggestions

- ★ Read through the poem out loud to yourself before performing it to the class, to help you decide where you could add emphasis and intonation to key words or lines.
- ★ When performing the poem, point to the part of the body mentioned in each line and make clear facial expressions and movements illustrating the different actions described.
- ★ Read the poem slowly, taking your time with each action word.
- ★ Clap or use a drum to create a simple musical beat for the last line.

Sequence Structure

This chart offers suggestions on the order and timings of exploring the story over a two-week period. However, please feel free to adapt the sessions to your own planning and suitable timings for your whole class or set groups.

Exploring the Poem

Tip: If possible, aim to perform the poem to or with the children regularly over the two-week period, or before any related activity, so that the children get to know the poem and its meaning well.

WEEK 1 (PHASE 1)	WEEKS 1–2 (PHASE 2)	WEEK 2 (PHASE 3)
Introduction to the poem	**Getting to know the poem**	**Performing the poem**
All sections could be done in one session or split over two or three sessions.	Aim to hold one or two sessions on getting to know the poem, each retelling the poem and then including your own choice of one or more activities.	This session could be rehearsed and performed at different times across the week.
1. **What do we know?** (15–20 minutes) 2. **Let's listen and talk** (approx. 30 minutes) **Extra consolidation activity:** ● What we can do (approx. 30 minutes)	3. **Let's get to know the poem** (10–15 minutes) **'Structure focus' activity:** ● Sequencing 'All About Me' (10–15 minutes) **'Vocabulary focus' activities:** ● Rhyming words (15–20 minutes) ● Action words (20–25 minutes) **'Phonics focus' activity:** ● Clapping syllable beats (10–15 minutes)	4. **Let's put on a performance** (20–30 minutes)

Literacy Activities

READING	WRITING	PHONICS WORK
● I spy ● Making body pairs ● Body books	● What I can do ● My body booklet ● Sensory writing	● Body spelling ● Dressing a snowman

Cross-curricular Activities

Adult-led activities:	Child-led activities:
● Moving puppets (Expressive Arts) ● Action songs, poems and stories (Communication and Language; Physical Development) ● Sensory fun (Physical Development; Communication and Language) ● Modelling a park (Expressive Arts; PSHE; Understanding the World)	● Being active (Physical Development) ● Fingerprint maths (Mathematics) ● Mirror paper plate faces (Expressive Arts; PSHE) ● Caring for each other (Communication and Language; PSHE; Understanding the World)

Sequence Assessment

● Communication and Language
● Reading
● Writing
● Review of the Big Picture

EXPLORING THE POEM

PHASE 1: Introduction to the poem

Session 1: What do we know?

Perform and sing the song 'Heads, Shoulders, Knees and Toes' with the children.

Then give prompts to assess the children's current knowledge about the names of parts of their body. For example: *Point to your head.*

- *Hold your ears.*
- *What other features are on our faces?*
- *Use your arms as if you are flying.*
- *Clap your hands above your head.*

- *Touch your elbows. How many elbows do you have?*
- *Pat your legs three times.*
- *Pat your knees.*
- *Touch your feet. How many feet do you have?*

Discuss the **Background Knowledge** given above. Then explain to the children that they are going to learn more about the different parts of their bodies and what they can do with them.

Session 2: Let's listen and talk

Remind the children briefly about the last session, and perform 'Heads, Shoulders, Knees and Toes' with them again, if you feel it is necessary. Display and introduce the poem 'All About Me '. Explain that this poem is also about the body, and about how we use it.

Show the **Storyteller** video for 'All About Me' on **Connect**, or read and perform it to the children. If you are performing the poem, use the poem text on **Connect** for hints and directions, and include props if required (see also the **Performance Ideas and Storytelling Suggestions** above).

After the reading, check that the children understand any new or difficult words (see **Key Vocabulary** above).

Ask questions to check the children's understanding of the poem and how they use body parts. These can be open to group discussion or children can pair

with talk partners before reporting back to the group. For example:

- *How does the poem say we can we use our heads?*
- *Show me how we can use our eyes.*
- *What kind of nice things do you hear with your ears?*
- *Who can make a snoring sound with their nose?*
- *How do we use our teeth? Has anyone lost teeth?*
- *What do we use when we want to hug someone?*
- *How do we use our knees and elbows?*
- *What does the poem say we can do with our 'two little feet'?*

Say the poem one more time. Slow down and encourage the children to predict and join in with saying the body parts and doing the actions.

Extra consolidation activity

What we can do

Explore the poem's actions, and other actions of these body parts, in more detail:

- Ask the children to try making different sounds (loud or soft, nice or boring) for their talk partners to hear and describe.
- Ask talk partners to discuss their favourite and least favourite smells.
- Ask the children to sing or whistle songs, for their talk partners to guess and/or with which they can join in.
- Ask the children to draw pictures of all the actions in the poem and that they have discussed.
- Create a display using a child-sized body shape cut out from craft paper, and add the pictures to the correct body part.

Differentiation: More confident writers could label the actions and/or body parts for the display.

EXPLORING THE POEM

PHASE 2: Getting to know the poem

Session 3: Let's get to know the poem 👥 👥

Remind the children of the poem and ask them what they remember about it. Retell the poem using the **Storyteller** video on **Connect**, or by reading it aloud to the class using the actions. Then retell or show the poem again, asking the children to join in with the actions and words.

After the retelling, choose focus activities to explore the poem in more depth.

'Structure focus' activity

Sequencing 'All About Me' 👥 👥

- Display the interactive activity 'All About Me'.
- Look at the figure on the screen and point to the top label: 'head'.
- Ask the children if they can remember what the head does in the poem.
- Then click on the label to show the poem line revealing this information.
- Repeat these steps for each label on the body.
- Once all the poem lines are revealed, read out the poem and encourage the children to join in with the actions.

'Vocabulary focus' activities

Rhyming words 👥 👥

- Look at the first two lines of the poem. Ask the children to say the words 'thinking' and 'blinking'.
- Emphasise the sounds that are the same: 'inking'. Explain that the two words **rhyme**: they have the same sound patterns at the end. Say them again slowly, so the children can hear the rhyme.
- Ask the children to join in with the rhyming words as you say the first two lines of the poem.
- Repeat for the other five pairs of rhyming lines. Point out that rhyming words can be short or long (using 'feet'/'beat' as an example of short (i.e. one-syllable) words rhyming.
- Say the poem again, and encourage the children to join you with all the rhyming words.

Differentiation: More confident children could explore other rhymes for the poem's end words.

Action words 👥 👥

- Read out the first two lines of the poem, putting emphasis on the six action words.
- Explain their purpose as action words to the children: they each describe doing something.
- Ask the children to do the actions as you say the words again.
- Go through the poem, one line at a time, and ask the children which words they think may be the action words. Ask them to perform the actions once the words have been identified.
- When you reach the final two lines, clap or use a percussion instrument so that the children can tap their feet to a 'musical beat'.

'Phonics focus' activity

Clapping syllable beats 👥 👥

- With the children sitting in a circle, use a drum to play a musical beat and ask them to clap along.
- Say 'head' and drum the one beat for the word. Ask the children to clap one beat.
- Say 'nodding' and drum the two beats for the word. Ask the children to clap two beats.
- Read through the poem, looking at all the action words in terms of their syllable beats.
- Next, ask a child in the circle to name an action (for example, look, shiver or tiptoe) and drum the syllable beat(s) for that word. Ask the children to clap along.
- Repeat, asking for an action word (or a body part) from each child in the circle.

EXPLORING THE POEM

PHASE 3: Performing the poem

Session 4: Let's put on a performance

Remind the children of their work so far. Show or retell the poem with the children, using facial expressions and miming the actions. Then create a performance of the poem by splitting the class into five or ten small groups or pairs:

- Allocate each group or pair a couple of lines to act out (or a line each, if ten groups/pairs have been formed). Omit the final rhyming couplet.

- Depending on the confidence of the children, they could do all the actions in their line(s) together or take turns, doing an action each.

- In preparation for the final pair of lines, ask the whole class to create a musical beat using percussion instruments: play different rhythmic beats and then ask the children which would work well for the poem.

- Ask the groups to stand in order, and then – as you read out the poem – to perform their actions at the appropriate time.

- Encourage the children to say the body parts from their lines, or the rhyming words at the ends of their lines, with you.

- When you reach the final two lines, the children should make actions using their feet such as hopping, dancing, skipping and jumping along with your beat.

- If possible, film the performance for the children to watch and enjoy.

Differentiation: More confident readers may wish to read their lines along with their performances or assist you in reading out the poem. Encourage as many children as possible to join in with this.

LITERACY ACTIVITIES

Reading

I spy

- Ask mixed-ability pairs to work on the interactive activity 'I Spy', choosing the right words for four items in a play-area scene.
- Discuss what other words with the initial-letter sound/s/could also be in the picture.

Differentiation: Write down other simple words for the play area, and ask more confident readers to use their sound and blending skills to decode the words.

Making body pairs

Cut out the tiles showing body parts and labels from Resource Sheet 1.1 for the children to use in a variety of reading games:

- Ask the children to match the labels with the images independently.
- Hand out one word or image card to each child at random, and ask the children to form pairs by finding the card that either labels or illustrates theirs.
- Ask the children (in pairs or independently) to draw a body and label it using the label cards.
- Give one child in each pair the image cards and the other the label cards. Ask the child with the label cards to start sounding out the words, concentrating on the initial letters, to request the correct image cards from their partner.

Differentiation: More confident readers may be able to add more word cards and body parts to the pack or to sound out the labels fully with greater accuracy and fluency.

Body books

- Ask pairs to share fun and interesting books about the body and physical activities (such as cycling, football, dancing or swimming).

Writing

What I can do

- Ask mixed-ability pairs to work on the interactive activity 'What I Can Do', adding the missing letters to complete each sentence.
- Once the activity is complete, ask the children to write out the sentences and draw the actions.

My body booklet

- Ask the children to compose simple sentences about their body verbally (for example, 'I have brown hair' or 'I have two hands') as you scribe the sentences for the children to copy or complete.
- Ask the children to illustrate their sentences.
- The children use their illustrated sentences to make their own body booklet.
- Write 'My body book by ... ' on each body book cover and then let the children write their names on it.
- Encourage them to share their books with others.

Sensory writing

- Write out labels for a full-body model, naming body parts and/or actions children can perform.
- Ask the children to use a variety of sensory craft materials (such as sand, fabric, glitter or pipe cleaners) to copy out the labels before you attach their creations to the model.

Phonics Work

Body spelling

- Write out these CVC action words taken from the poem: 'nod', 'hug', 'run' and 'tap'.
- Ask the children to create large letter cards for the letters in these words (creating two cards each for the letters 'n' and 'u').
- Read out a word from the list, sounding out each letter. Ask the children holding the correct letter cards to step forward, and then ask the children to help you to place them in order.
- Ask the class to sound out each letter and blend them together to make the word.
- Repeat for the remaining words, making sure that all the children get a chance to use their skills in sounding and blending letters.

Differentiation: More confident children could look at model blending CVCC, CCVC and CCVCC words from the poem, such as 'help', 'bend', 'kick', 'kiss', 'clap', 'think', 'blink' and 'smell'.

Dressing a snowman

- Ask mixed-ability pairs to work on the interactive activity 'Dressing a Snowman', sounding out the labels and dragging the items to dress the snowman.
- Once the activity has been completed, point to different items and ask the children what they are, encouraging them to sound out and say the words.

CROSS-CURRICULAR ACTIVITIES

Adult-led activities 👥

Moving puppets (Expressive Arts; Communication and Language)

- Cut out the shapes from Resource Sheet 1.2.
- Ask the children to decorate them and then assemble the bodies using split pins.
- Discuss the different moving parts of the puppet, and the actions it can perform.

Action songs, poems and stories (Communication and Language; Physical Development)

- Throughout the two weeks, sing different action songs with the children (for example, 'If You're Happy and You Know It', 'The Hokey Cokey' and 'Dingle Dangle Scarecrow'), and read action poems and picture books (such as *Zoom!*).
- Ask the children to join in and then discuss the actions.

Sensory fun (Physical Development; Communication and Language)

- Set up various sensory activities to enable the children to explore and discuss their different senses. These could include identifying objects they feel in bags, guessing what is making different sounds or naming different foods from their scents.

Modelling a park (Expressive Arts; PSHE; Understanding the World)

Create a large model of a park:

- Discuss with the children what would be in the park (for example, slides, swings, benches, a pond, and so on).
- Ask the children to create models or card pictures to add to their park.
- Use the model to discuss what activities they like to do in the park, and what parts of their bodies these use.

Child-led activities 👥 👥 👤

Being active (Physical Development)

Set out equipment that encourages children to use their bodies (for example, bean bags, soft climbing blocks and pop-up tunnels) and ask them to name the activities they perform.

Fingerprint maths (Mathematics)

Write a number on a piece of paper and ask the children to make the correct number of fingerprints under it. Use these sheets for assistance with adding.

Mirror paper plate faces (Expressive Arts; PSHE)

- Give talk partners a paper plate each.
- Encourage children to look at themselves closely in a mirror and then to discuss their different features with their partners.
- Then ask them to use a range of craft materials to recreate their faces on their plates.

Caring for each other (Communication and Language; PSHE; Understanding the World)

- Set up role-play that encourages children to explore visits to people and places that deal with the body (for example, a doctors' or dentists' surgery, an opticians', and so on). Ask them to explain why they are there, naming a body part and an activity they wish to complete.

SEQUENCE ASSESSMENT

Communication and Language

- Does the child listen and respond to discussion about the poem?
- Does the child listen to and join in with the retelling of the poem?
- Does the child use talk to organise, sequence and clarify thinking and ideas about the poem and the related poem activities?
- Does the child show evidence of extending their vocabulary?

Reading

- Can the child recognise rhythm in the poem's lines?
- Can the child anticipate key words and rhymes in the poem?
- Can the child hear initial sounds in words relating to different parts of the body?
- Can the child segment and blend sounds in CVC/CVCC words relating to the body?
- Can the child begin to read simple sentences?

Writing

- Can the child write labels for parts of the body?
- Can the child segment and blend sounds in CVC/CVCC words relating to the body?
- Can the child use some clearly identifiable letters to communicate meaning, representing some sounds correctly and in sequence?
- Can the child begin to write simple sentences?

Review of the Big Picture

At the end of this sequence, discuss with the children what they liked about the poem 'All About Me'. Ask: *Which lines did you like most? What have you learnt about the parts of the body and how we use them? Which action words did you like most, and why?*

Encourage each child to show and explain examples of their writing and reading achievements, and any cross-curricular activities they enjoyed.

Use the 'Pupil observation chart' to record each child's responses and attainments.

SEQUENCE 2 Ourselves: What I Can Do

TERM 1 (AUTUMN): 1st half term

Main Topic:	Ourselves
Subtopic:	What I Can Do
Text Type:	Poem
Main Source Text:	'Show and Tell' by James Carter, from *A First Poetry Book* edited by Pie Corbett and Gaby Morgan (ISBN 978-0-330-54374-3)
Extra Source Text:	'Going Through Old Photos' by Michael Rosen, from *The Puffin Book of Fantastic First Poems* edited by June Crebbin (ISBN 978-0-141-30898-2)
Approximate Duration:	Two weeks

Big Picture

During this sequence, children will listen to the alphabet list poem 'Show and Tell' and discuss its meaning, structure and vocabulary as a group. They will join in with the poem using actions, and will enact it.

The children will explore alphabet lists and alphabetical order and, through a range of supportive activities, will have the opportunity to find out more about themselves, their families and their interests through song, role-play, class graphs and craft (creating collages and paper quilts).

Phonics Focuses

The children will investigate initial-letter sounds, read and write simple CVC words, and learn and recognise the alphabet.

Learning Outcomes: See 'Learning Outcomes' Chart, on pages xi–xiv.

Key Vocabulary: 'show and tell', West Ham, France, acorns, cloak, wizard

Home Links

Encourage children to:

- collect photographs of different family members
- share and discuss what they would like to say in 'show and tell' sessions
- say the initial-letter sounds of objects they see around their home
- look at the alphabet and sing the alphabet rhyme.

Resources Required

Workbook Pages: 4–10
Resource Sheets 2.1–2.2: Rhyming Words (Part A); Rhyming Words (Part B)

General Resources:

- A small shell
- A sticking plaster
- Craft paper
- Various cut-out images from magazines or newspapers, or printed from a computer
- Copies of the alphabet
- Craft materials (e.g. modelling dough, sand, seeds, textiles, macaroni, glitter, paints, pens)
- Long card or paper streamers
- Small-world toys (human figures, lorries, ships)

Background Knowledge

Explain to the children that:

- the poem 'Show and Tell' illustrates a speaking and listening activity that encourages children to share their news, skills, hobbies or interests to their class or within a group
- this activity is intended to allow them to celebrate their individuality and grow their self-esteem
- if they feel uncomfortable taking part in a 'show and tell' presentation they may choose to talk in pairs or groups, using a puppet or with the help of an adult.

Performance Ideas and Storytelling Suggestions

★ Read through the poem out loud to yourself before performing it to the class, to help you decide where you could add emphasis and intonation to key words or lines (for example, emphasising the names of the children and the end rhyming words).

★ When performing the poem, use facial expressions and, where possible, mime the actions. You may also choose to use puppets to help illustrate the poem.

Sequence Structure

This chart offers suggestions on the order and timings of exploring the story over a two-week period. However, please feel free to adapt the sessions to your own planning and suitable timings for your whole class or set groups.

Exploring the Poem

Tip: If possible, aim to perform the poem to or with the children regularly over the two-week period, or before any related activity, so that the children get to know the poem and its meaning well.

WEEK 1 (PHASE 1)	WEEKS 1–2 (PHASE 2)	WEEK 2 (PHASE 3)
Introduction to the poem	**Getting to know the poem**	**Performing the poem**
All sections could be done in one session or split over two or three sessions.	Aim to hold one or two sessions on getting to know the poem, each retelling the poem and then including your own choice of activities.	This session could be rehearsed and performed at different times across the week.
1. What do we know? (15–20 minutes) **2. Let's listen and talk** (approx. 30 minutes) **Extra consolidation activity:** • Our own 'show and tell' (approx. 20 minutes)	**3. Let's get to know the poem** (10–15 minutes) **'Structure focus' activities:** • Finding the alphabet (approx. 10 minutes) • Show or tell? (10–15 minutes) **'Vocabulary focus' activities:** • Matching rhyming words (approx. 20 minutes) • Composing a 'show and tell' alphabet poem (approx. 30 minutes) **'Phonics focus' activity:** • Initial-letter sounds (approx. 10 minutes)	**4. Let's put on a performance** (20–30 minutes)

Literacy Activities

READING	WRITING	PHONICS WORK
• Show and tell 'p' objects	• How did Bella fall?	• Matching initials
• Matching labels to objects	• Name writing	• Alphabet-sorting streamers
• Alphabet displays	• 'This Is Me' booklet	• A CVC poem

Cross-curricular Activities

Adult-led activities:
- Photo albums (PSHE)
- Graphing our favourite activities (Mathematics)
- 'Show and tell' (Communication and Language)
- Activity quilting (PSHE; Expressive Arts)
- Collection corner (PSHE; Communication and Language)

Child-led activities:
- Name art (Expressive Arts)
- Collages (Expressive Arts; Communication and Language; PSHE)
- Favourite songs and rhymes (Communication and Language; Expressive Arts)
- Small-world 'show and tell' (Communication and Language; PSHE)

Sequence Assessment

- Communication and Language
- Reading
- Writing
- Review of the Big Picture

EXPLORING THE POEM

PHASE 1: Introduction to the poem

Session 1: What do we know?

Encourage children to discuss any past experiences of 'show and tell' sessions in their pre-school groups, and then model a 'show and tell' session, focusing on yourself.

- Start with a 'show' example (for example, something or things you have made, collected or can do). Use your hands to indicate the action of 'showing' to help the children understand what you are doing. Explain clearly what you are showing and why you want to show it to others.

- Now model a 'tell' example (for example, describing an experience or some knowledge you would like to share). Point to your mouth or mime speaking to indicate the action of 'telling'.

Discuss the **Background Knowledge** given above. Then explain to the children that they are going to use the poem as a prompt for fun activities to find out more about each other and themselves.

Session 2: Let's listen and talk

Display the illustrated poem ('Show and Tell 1') on the whiteboard, and introduce it by holding up a small shell and a sticking plaster.

Read out the first two lines of the poem, and highlight that one child *shows* a shell (use hand actions to present the shell) and another child *tells* about how she fell down (use hand actions to point to your mouth or mime speaking).

Show the **Storyteller** video for 'Show and Tell' on **Connect**, or read it aloud from the whiteboard. If you are performing the poem, use hand gestures as appropriate to act it out (see the **Performance Ideas and Storytelling Suggestions** above).

After the reading, check that the children understand any new or difficult words (see **Key Vocabulary** above).

Ask questions to check the children's understanding of the poem. These can be open to group discussion or children can pair with talk partners before reporting back to the group. For example:

- *Who did Georgia talk about?*
- *What was Sarah's frog made from?*
- *Who was learning to swim?*
- *Why do you think Zoe didn't want to do 'show and tell'?*

- *Which 'show and tell' did you like most? Why?*

Focus on different 'show and tell' activities in the poem and encourage the children to draw images of the objects, or act out the actions, to help them to visualise the events. Then encourage the children to explore the presentations further through group or pair discussion, providing further prompts if necessary. For example:

- *How do you think Bella might have fallen?*
- *How do you think Faron's daddy would have got to France?*
- *What do you think Kieran may have done that was naughty?*
- *How many acorns do you think Vinny could bring in?*

Finally, point out that each 'show and tell' presentation in the poem is different. Highlight that we are all different, and that it is good to share who we are, what we like and what we can do with others.

Say the poem one more time. Slow down and encourage the children to predict and join in with the names of the children or the rhyming words at the end of the lines.

Extra consolidation activity

Our own 'show and tell'

- Ask talk partners to discuss what they would like to *show* the class before inviting feedback from the whole class.
- Now ask talk partners to discuss what they would like to *tell* the class about (perhaps a visit or trip) before inviting feedback from the whole class.
- If possible, arrange a 'show and tell' session for the children's suggestions, to take place at a later date.

EXPLORING THE POEM

PHASE 2: Getting to know the poem

Session 3: Let's get to know the poem 👥 👥

Show the children the shell and the sticking plaster again, and remind them of the poem. Ask them what they remember about it. Retell the poem using the **Storyteller** video on **Connect**, or by displaying the illustrated poem ('Show and Tell 1') on the whiteboard and reading it aloud using actions, where appropriate. Then retell the poem again, asking the children to join in with words and/or actions.

After the second retelling, choose focus activities to explore the poem in more depth.

'Structure focus' activities

Finding the alphabet 👥 👥

- Display the poem text ('Show and Tell') on the whiteboard.
- Point at or highlight the capital letters at the beginning of each line.
- Explain that this is an alphabet poem because the lines start with the letters of the alphabet in order.
- Point to the starting letters, and read them out using an alphabet rhyme (or other alphabet-learning method) that is familiar to the children.
- Encourage the children to repeat the alphabet with you.
- Point out that we use a capital letter at the beginning of each of our names. Ask the children what letter starts their names.

Differentiation: More confident children may be able to air-draw or write their names' capital letters.

Show or tell? 👥 👥

- Display the interactive activity 'Show or Tell?'. Point to the 'Show' and 'Tell' circles.
- Look at the various images and link them to lines from the poem. Discuss whether the child is 'showing' or 'telling' in each case.
- Drag the answers to the correct circle.

'Vocabulary focus' activities

Matching rhyming words 👥 👥

- Before the activity, cut out all the word cards from Resource Sheets 2.1 and 2.2.
- Read the first two lines of the poem to the children, with emphasis on the two end-of-line words, 'shell and 'fell'. Note that 'shell ' and 'fell' rhyme: they end with the same sound. Tell the children they're going to help you match other rhyming pairs from the poem.
- Put six children in a line, and give each a word card from Resource Sheet 2.1 to hold up.
- Read out each word, asking the children to repeat the word after you.
- Set out the word cards from Resource Sheet 2.2. Read a word and ask the children to match it to its correct rhyming word. (You may wish to read out each held word again).
- Once a rhyming pair is made, let a child take the loose card and stand by its rhyming partner.
- Once all pairs are made, read out all the rhyming words with the children. Then read out the poem and ask the children to hold up their words when they hear them.

Differentiation: Ask the children to suggest more rhyming words to go with the six pairs. Write them on cards for the children to hold.

Composing a 'show and tell' alphabet poem 👥 👥

- On A3 paper, write the names in the poem vertically, in alphabetical order, asking for verbal help from the children. Emphasise the initial-letter sounds.
- Pass around a bag of various cut-out images and let children take out one for each name on the paper.
- With the children's verbal assistance, create new lines for the poem, using the existing names and the object or an event it suggests (for example, 'Amber told about her hens'). The lines needn't rhyme.
- Read the poem back with the children.
- Add the images to the poem and display it.

EXPLORING THE POEM

'Phonics focus' activity

Initial-letter sounds

- Display the interactive activity 'Initial-Letter sounds'.
- Note that some of the names from the poem are missing their first initial letter.
- Point to the initial letters at the side of the screen and say each one.
- Click on the first name to hear it. Ask the children what the sound of the first letter is, and what the letter is called.
- Ask the children to assist you in dragging the correct initial letter to each name.
- Repeat these steps until all names have been completed.

Differentiation: Encourage faster children to sound out other names from the poem.

PHASE 3: Performing the poem

Session 4: Let's put on a performance

Over the week, encourage the children to explore the poem through role-play by asking them to act out some of the various activities outlined in the poem (for example, falling over; going to see a friend or family member; travelling to France on a coach, airplane, ferry or car; watching a football match; singing or dancing; eating an ice cream; telling a joke or saying a nursery rhyme). Props could also be made or brought in for assistance.

During the final session, remind the children of their work so far. Show the poem again using the **Storyteller** video on **Connect**, or retell it with the children from the whiteboard. Then ask the children to work together to create a performance of the poem.

- Allocate groups or pairs of children sets of two rhyming lines to perform.
- Ask each group to prepare a presentation of their lines. This could be:
  - a picture or puppet of their poem characters, with their names and initial letters written out and decorated
  - a mime or hand gestures
  - a role-play (as explored over the week).

- Ask the groups to stand in order, and then – as you read out the poem – to give their performances or presentations at the appropriate time.
- Encourage the children to say the names at the beginnings of their lines, or the rhyming words at the ends of their lines, with you.
- If possible, film the performance for the children to watch and enjoy.

Differentiation: More confident readers may wish to read their lines along with their performances or assist you in reading out the poem.

LITERACY ACTIVITIES

Reading

Show and tell 'p' objects

- Ask mixed-ability pairs to work on the interactive activity 'Show and Tell 'p' Objects', clicking on the items that start with the same sound.

Differentiation: Ask more confident readers to work out the initial sounds for the other items.

Matching labels to objects

- Show the children a set of items that could be used in a 'show and tell' session (such as model cars, a doll, buttons, an apple and a stamp).
- Write out word labels for these items, with the initial letters highlighted.
- Ask the children to say the initial letters to help them to work out which card matches with which object.

Differentiation: Encourage more confident readers to sound out and blend some other phonemes on the labels, to help them to work out the words.

Alphabet displays

- Create and display visual alphabets using images of various objects (such as food, activities, animals, and so on).
- Ask the children to position the correct initial letter under each image and put the alphabet in order.

Writing

Sequencing: How did Bella fall?

- Ask mixed-ability pairs to use the interactive activity 'How Did Bella Fall?', selecting the correct words to complete the short sentences.

Name writing

- Write out the children's names for them, and then encourage them to join you in sounding them out.
- Suggest the children try to air-write each letter in their name.
- Then encourage them to practise writing out their names in a variety of ways (for example, using modelling dough, sand, seeds or textiles).

'This is me' booklet

- Ask each child to create their own booklet about who they are and what they like.

- Write five incomplete set sentences on each page, such as:
  - My name is _____.
  - I am _____ years old.
  - I live in a _____.
  - I am good at _____.
  - I like playing with _____.
- Ask the children to complete the sentences verbally and write the initial letter of their added word before you complete their responses as a scribe.
- Ask the children to share their booklets within a 'show and tell' session.

Differentiation: More confident writers may be able to help sound out and, with guidance, write out the words they have contributed.

Phonics Work

Matching initials

- Use the interactive activity 'Match the Initials' to encourage children to say and match the initial letters to the CVC words, with picture support.

Differentiation: More confident children could verbally sound out and write down more CVC words using similar VC spelling patterns.

Alphabet-sorting streamers

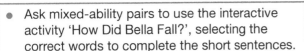

- Give groups or pairs of children a set of letters (for example, a–b or a–d) and a set of various images. Encourage them to find images of things that start with their alphabet letters.
- Then ask the children to stick their images onto a long streamer in alphabetical order, saying the initial sounds as they do so.
- Hold a 'show and tell' session for the children to share their work, and display the streamers in order to create a whole alphabet, sticking the letters above them.

Differentiation: Encourage confident children to try to recognise other sounds within the words.

A CVC poem

- Write down the CVC name 'Ben' and sound it out with the children.
- Ask for suggestions of, and then write down, other words ending in 'e-n' (such as 'den', 'hen', 'Ken' and 'ten').
- With the children, create a one-line poem using some of the words: for example, 'Ben has a hen in a den.'
- Repeat this process using alternative CVC combinations based on children's phonic knowledge, to create a new poem.

CROSS-CURRICULAR ACTIVITIES

Adult-led activities 👥👤

Photo albums (PSHE)

- Look at the extra source text, 'Going Through Old Photos' by Michael Rosen.
- Ask the children to bring in family photos, or draw pictures, of different members of their families and produce a class album or picture display. If some families live outside of the UK, display images of these countries for the children to see, too.

Graphing our favourite activities (Mathematics)

- Present the children with a selection of popular activities. Encourage groups to discuss which activity they (would) enjoy most and why.
- Draw a bar graph or pictograph and ask children for their responses to complete it. Give each child a square sticker to add to the graph. Help the children discuss and count the results. Which activity was the most popular?

'Show and tell' (Communication and Language)

- Try to include a regular 'show and tell' session each week, or every other week, for the children to share their news and achievements.

Activity quilting (PSHE; Expressive Arts)

- Give each child a quilt shape made from coloured craft paper. Ask children to draw images of things they like to do. Put all the shapes together to make a large activity quilt for display.

Collection corner (PSHE; Communication and Language)

- Set up a collection corner where children can bring in items to create class collections (such as acorns, leaves, cards or shells).
- Allow them to create collections of classroom objects here too (for example, by arranging toys).

Child-led activities 👥👤 👤👤 👤

Name art (Expressive Arts)

- Create name cards for each child, making the initial letters large.
- Allow children to select their own materials to decorate their cards, asking them to make the initial letter their focus.

Collages (Expressive Arts; Communication and Language; PSHE)

- Ask the children's parents or carers to help them create a paper collage of their life and interests, including images of their hobbies and interests, and pictures of family, friends and pets.
- Use the collages for a 'show and tell' session.

Favourite songs and rhymes (Communication and Language; Expressive arts)

- Over the two weeks, let each child have the opportunity to choose a favourite song or rhyme and encourage everyone to join in performing it. Discuss why this is a favourite.

Small-world 'show and tell' (Communication and Language; PSHE)

- Ask children to use small-world toys to practise presenting their (or characters') news and skills.

SEQUENCE ASSESSMENT

Communication and Language

- Does the child listen and respond to discussion about the poem?
- Does the child listen and join in with the retelling of the poem?
- Does the child use talk to organise, sequence and clarify thinking and ideas about the poem and the related poem activities?
- Does the child show evidence of extending their vocabulary?

Reading

- Can the child hear and say initial sounds?
- Can the child hear rhythm in spoken words?
- Can the child recognise familiar words and their names?
- Can the child link sounds to letters?
- Can the child name and sound the letters of the alphabet?
- Can the child begin to read words and simple sentences?
- Can the child segment and blend sounds in simple CVC words?

Writing

- Can the child write something that continues a rhyming string?
- Can the child segment and blend sounds in simple CVC words?
- Can the child link sounds to letters?
- Can the child name and sound the letters of the alphabet?
- Can the child write their own name?

Review of the Big Picture

At the end of this sequence, discuss with the children what they liked about the poem 'Show and Tell'. Ask: *Which 'show and tell' item or words or phrases did you like? What 'show and tell' activity did you enjoy the most? What have you shared about yourselves with others? What letter sounds do you know, and can you say your alphabet?*

Encourage each child to show and explain examples of their writing and reading achievements, and any cross-curricular activities they enjoyed.

Use the 'Pupil observation chart' to record each child's responses and attainments.

SEQUENCE 3 Ourselves: Family and Friendship

TERM 1 (AUTUMN): 1st half term

Main Topic:	Ourselves
Subtopic:	Family and Friendship
Text Type:	Story
Main Source Text:	*Mog and Bunny* by Judith Kerr (ISBN 978-0-007-17130-9)
Extra Source Text:	*Sharing A Shell* by Julia Donaldson (ISBN 978-1-405-02048-0)
Approximate Duration:	Two weeks

Big Picture

During this sequence, children will listen to the story 'Mog and Bunny' and discuss its messages, structure and vocabulary as a group. They will also have the opportunity to explore the characters and events through role-play.

Through a range of supportive activities, the children will have the opportunity to investigate the themes of friendship and attachment in more depth.

Phonics Focuses

The children will investigate CVC words such as 'Mog' and 'cat', and their VC spelling patterns. They will also use initial letters to help them to read and write simple words.

Learning Outcomes: See 'Learning Outcomes' Chart, on pages xi–xiv.

Key Vocabulary: Bunny, present, radiator, cosy, horrible, threatened

Home Links

Encourage children to:

- talk about friendships with their families and friends
- think of ways they can be a friend to others
- take or draw a picture of their favourite toy to bring in to share with the class.

Resources Required

Workbook Pages: 6–11, 29–30

Resource Sheet 3.1: Bunny Toy Template

General Resources:

- A soft toy
- A range of different toys and other small objects
- Labels
- Felt, thread, needles, stuffing and fabric pens (or craft paper, scissors and felt pens)
- Paint and other craft materials
- Paper plates
- Small-world toys (human figures, animals, toys)

Background Knowledge

Explain to the children that:

- 'Mog and Bunny' is one of a series of stories about Mog the cat, and her life with Debbie, Nicky and their parents
- this story focuses on three areas; having a special toy, losing something special and being good friends to each other.

Discuss with the children what they understand by the concepts of friendship, family and attachment.

Performance Ideas and Storytelling Suggestions

★ Read through the story out loud to yourself before reading it to the class, to help you decide where you could add emphasis and intonation to key words or lines (for example, using different voices or inflections for the different characters).

★ When reading the story, stop at various points to ask questions that will encourage predictions (for example, *Where could Mog be? What will the children do? Where was Bunny?*)

Sequence Structure

This chart offers suggestions on the order and timings of exploring the story over a two-week period. However, please feel free to adapt the sessions to your own planning and suitable timings for your whole class or set groups.

Exploring the Story

Tip: If possible, aim to read or show the story to the children regularly over the two-week period, or before any related activity, so that the children get to know the story and its messages well.

WEEK 1 (PHASE 1)	WEEKS 1–2 (PHASE 2)	WEEKS 1–2 (PHASE 3)
Introduction to the story	**Getting to know the story**	**Exploring the story through role-play**
All sections could be done in one session or split over two or three sessions.	Aim to hold one or two sessions on getting to know the story, each retelling the story and then including your own choice of activities.	Aim to hold one or two sessions at different times across the two-week period.
1. **What do we know?** (15–20 minutes) 2. **Let's listen and talk** (approx. 30 minutes) **Extra consolidation activity:** ● Toys from 'Mog and Bunny' (approx. 20 minutes)	3. **Let's get to know the story** (10–15 minutes) **'Structure focus' activity:** ● Story sequencing (approx. 15 minutes) **'Vocabulary focus' activity:** ● Playing with Bunny (15–20 minutes) **'Comprehension focus' activity:** ● Friendship chart (approx. 20 minutes) **'Phonics focus' activity:** ● Where is Bunny? (approx. 10 minutes)	4. **Let's perform a role-play** ● Being Mog (approx. 30 minutes) ● Losing Bunny (approx. 30 minutes) ● Mog's friends (approx. 30 minutes)

Literacy Activities

READING	WRITING	PHONICS WORK
● Matching lost objects ● Mog's adventures ● Treasure hunt!	● Pet sentences ● Mog's new adventure ● Our friendship chain	● Mog's CVC words ● Initial sounds for toys

Cross-curricular Activities

Adult-led activities:

- Making a friend (Expressive Arts)
- Songs and rhymes (Communication and Language; Expressive Arts)
- Friendship circle (Communication and Language; PSHE)
- Hide and seek (Communication and Language; PSHE)

Child-led activities:

- Friendship pictures (Expressive Arts; PSHE)
- Friendship dance and movement (Expressive Arts; PSHE)
- Small-world friendships (Communication and Language; PSHE)
- My favourite toy (Communication and Language; PSHE)

Sequence Assessment

- Communication and Language
- Reading
- Writing
- Review of the Big Picture

EXPLORING THE STORY

PHASE 1: Introduction to the story

Session 1: What do we know?

Make a 'Bunny' soft toy or a paper puppet using Resource sheet 3.1. Show 'Bunny' to the children and explain that it's the favourite toy of a cat called Mog. Encourage the children to talk about their favourite toys. Ask questions to help each child focus on why their toy is special. For example:

- *What do you like about your toy?*
- *How do you like to play with your toy?*
- *Does it have a name?*
- *Why do you call it that?*

Then ask children about any pets they have. Ask similar questions.

Explain that Mog the cat has two good friends who play with him and look after him. Ask open questions to encourage the children to talk about their friends. For example:

- *What do you like about your friends?*
- *What do you like doing with them?*

Discuss the **Background Knowledge** given above. Then explain to the children that they are going to learn more about friendship, family and attachment from the characters Mog and Bunny, and Mog's owners, Debbie and Nicky.

Session 2: Let's listen and talk

Introduce the story *Mog and Bunny* by showing children the first image of Mog and Bunny from the **Storyteller** video on **Connect**. Ask them which character they think is Mog, and which is Bunny. Focus on Mog's expression and ask the children how they think Mog feels about Bunny.

Show the **Storyteller** video for *Mog and Bunny* on **Connect**, or read the story yourself (see the **Performance Ideas and Storytelling Suggestions** above).

After the reading, check that the children understand any new or difficult words (see **Key Vocabulary** above).

Ask questions to check the children's understanding of the story. These can be open to group discussion or children can pair with talk partners before reporting back to the group. For example:

- *What did Nicky give Mog as a present?*
- *What kind of things did Mog do with Bunny?*

- *Where was Bunny put when it got wet?*
- *Why didn't Nicky and Debbie's mum and dad like Bunny?*
- *Why was Mog outside in the rain?*
- *How did the children get Mog to come inside?*
- *How did Nicky and Debbie look after Mog and Bunny?*
- *What did you like about the story?*

Look at the pictures again, and prompt the children to comment on how Bunny changes from a clean, new toy to a shabby, dirty, earless one. Ask them why they think Mog still loves Bunny, even when Bunny is dirty and earless. Link the discussion to that about children's own favourite toys, and why they love them.

Extra consolidation activity

Toys from 'Mog and Bunny'

- Show the illustrations again. Ask the children what toys they think are Nicky's and Debbie's favourites. (Nicky's is a bear; Debbie's is a rag doll.)
- Ask talk partners to discuss which toy they would prefer (Bunny, the bear or the doll).
- Then ask them to discuss names for their chosen toy, bear and doll, before they feed back their ideas to the class.
- Write the names on the board, sounding out the initial letters.

EXPLORING THE STORY

PHASE 2: Getting to know the story

Session 3: Let's get to know the story 👥 👥

Show the children a rabbit toy or puppet again, and remind them of the story. Ask them what they remember about it. Retell the story using the **Storyteller** video on **Connect**, or reading the story again yourself.

After the retelling, choose focus activities to explore the story in more depth.

'Structure focus' activity

Story sequencing 👥 👥

- Display the interactive activity 'Mog and Bunny Story Sequence'.
- Point and listen to the mixed-up summaries of parts of the story and discuss each one (and its order in the story) with the children.
- Encourage the children to retell the events of the story, to help you to order the images.
- Once the images are in the correct sequence, encourage the children to retell the story again, in their own words, or to a talk partner.

'Vocabulary focus' activity

Playing with Bunny 👥 👥

- Show the illustrations of Mog playing with Bunny.
- Discuss what Mog was doing with Bunny. (Mog looks at, holds, carries, lifts, throws, jumps on, sniffs, chews, eats with and washes Bunny.)
- Model a sentence verbally for the children to repeat (for example, 'Mog hugs Bunny').
- Let the children use the sentence structure to create new sentences verbally, about how Mog plays with Bunny.
- Ask the children to draw pictures of their favourite one of these activities.

Differentiation: Encourage more confident children to write, under their pictures: 'Mog likes to play with Bunny.' All children might have a go with appropriate adult or word bank support.

'Comprehension focus' activity

Friendship chart 👥 👥

- Stick printed pictures of Mog, Nicky and Debbie, or write their names, in the middle of a large sheet of craft paper.
- Ask the children to suggest different ways that Debbie and Nicky were good friends to Mog (for example, they gave him a present, played games with him, took care of Bunny, missed him, helped him to find Bunny and got him dry).
- As the children make their suggestions, draw or note these down around the three characters.
- Use the chart to discuss further what makes a good friend.

'Phonics focus' activity

Where is Bunny? 👥 👥

- Display the interactive activity 'Where is Bunny?'.
- Ask the children to help you find Bunny (who is hiding behind an object such as a bin, pen or sock).
- Ask the children to sound out and blend the phonemes to read the name of each object that could be hiding Bunny.
- Once all the words have been read out, ask different children which object may be hiding Bunny. Click the object to see if Bunny is there.

Differentiation: For less confident children, model sounding out the words.

EXPLORING THE STORY

PHASE 3: Exploring the story through role-play

Session 4: Let's perform a role-play 👥 👥

Over the two weeks, encourage the children to explore the story through role-play.

During the final session, remind the children of their work so far. Show the story again using the **Storyteller** video on **Connect**, or retell it with the children from the whiteboard. Then ask the children to work together to explore an element of the story in more depth. Focuses for different groups could include:

Being Mog

- Ask the children to talk about cats, and how they play and move. Encourage children with pet cats to share their own experiences.
- Ask the children to imagine that they are Mog. Suggest different actions and movements (for example, playing with Bunny, eating and drinking, sleeping, pouncing and running) and sounds (for example, purring, meowing and howling).

Losing Bunny

- Ask the children to imagine that they are Mog, and have lost Bunny.
- Give instructions about actions they could perform (for example, 'look under the table', 'look in the toy box', 'look outside').
- Afterwards, discuss with the children how Mog must have felt, and why he sat in the rain until help came.

Mog's friends

- Discuss with the children the different ways Nicky and Debbie looked after Mog during the day.
- Put the children into threes, with one pretending to be Mog and the other two becoming Nicky and Debbie.
- Ask Nicky and Debbie to look after Mog, and allow different threes to share ideas.
- Then remind the children what happened when Mog lost Bunny, and ask them to act out the story from the moment it started raining.

LITERACY ACTIVITIES

Reading

Matching lost objects

- Ask mixed-ability pairs to work on the interactive activity 'Match the Lost Object', reading the CVC words and matching the objects to their owners.

Differentiation: Children should peer-support using the sounds they know, with the more confident readers modeling blending. Focus on the initial highlighted letter sounds of each object.

Mog's adventures

- Collect more stories about Mog and share them with the children.
- Have them available in the reading corner for the children to look at and share.

Treasure hunt!

- Hide toys or other small objects around the room, with word labels attached to them.
- Give mixed-ability pairs a list of objects to sound out and read.
- Ask them to hunt and find the objects with the matching word cards.
- Once all the objects are found, ask the children share their treasures with the class by reading out their words.

Writing

Pet sentences

- Ask mixed-ability pairs to complete the interactive activity 'Pet Sentences', completing the sentences by selecting the correct words after an audio prompt.

Differentiation: Ask more confident writers to write the sentences out and draw pictures with them.

Mog's new adventure

- Suggest that groups make up new stories about Nicky and Debbie helping Mog.
- Use questioning and talk partners to begin the process (for example, *What is Mog doing? Where is she? How could she get into trouble? How do Nicky and Debbie help her? How does the story end?*)
- Once the story has been planned, create a storyboard with the children.
- Ask each child to say a sentence for each part of the story.

- Write these down on the storyboard, encouraging children to help you to sound out and blend certain words.

Differentiation: More confident children could create their own storyboards and record their sentences electronically with adult/phonics and word bank support.

Our friendship chain

- Draw around the hand of each child and cut it out.
- Encourage the children to write their names on the hands, helping them to recognise and sound out familiar letter sounds.
- Let the children use colouring materials to decorate their hands.
- Collect all the hands and arrange them in a circular pattern or a long, horizontal chain.
- Write a label to go with it: 'Our friendship chain'.
- Use the chain to discuss friendship further.

Differentiation: Less confident writers may need prompting and encouraging to sound out and spell the tricky parts of their name. Children may have access to name cards to check against.

Phonics Work

Mog's CVC words

- Ask mixed-ability pairs to work on the interactive activity 'Mog's CVC Words', listening to and sorting CVC words that end with the VC patterns 'un' or 'at'.

Differentiation: Encourage more confident children to think of other words that end with 'at' or 'un', or give them another set of CVC word patterns to sound out and sort.

Initial sounds for toys

- Show a selection of different toys, and provide letter cards that could be put together to make the name of each toy.
- Point to a toy and ask the children what it is. Ask them to say the sound for the initial letter of the word. Then ask the children to find that letter card and put it by the toy.
- Repeat for the other toys.
- Finally, suggest that the children give each toy a name. Ask them to say the initial letter of the name, and to choose the correct letter card.

Differentiation: Encourage more confident children to sound out and blend the letters of more complex names.

CROSS-CURRICULAR ACTIVITIES

Adult-led activities 👥

Making a friend (Expressive Arts)

Using Resource Sheet 3.1 ('Bunny Toy Template'), assist children in making their own new soft toys:
- Cut out the template from two pieces of felt or cloth.
- Sew the two shapes together, leaving an opening through which children can add stuffing.
- Encourage children to stuff their toys and draw on faces.
- Sew up the opening in each toy.

(If this process is not practical, cut the template from paper and create paper puppets.)

Songs and rhymes (Communication and Language; Expressive Arts)

- Teach various songs and rhymes that focus on friendship or toys. For example:
  - We Can Play on the Big Bass Drum
  - If You're Happy and You Know It
  - Miss Polly had a Dolly

Friendship circle (Communication and Language; PSHE)

- Ask the children to sit in a circle.
- Ask each child in turn what they think a friend is, and write down their answers on a display.
- Add images of the children onto the display to celebrate examples of good friendship.
- Ask groups or pairs to act out a friendship scenario, to give an example of each answer.

Hide and seek (Communication and Language; PSHE)

- Play a game of hide and seek, using a hidden toy. Ask the children to look around the classroom for it, or give them directions to follow.

Child-led activities 👥 👥

Friendship pictures (Expressive Arts; PSHE)

- Give talk partners a paper plate each.
- Encourage children to look at each other closely and then to use a range of craft materials to recreate the face of their partner on their plate.

Friendship dance and movement (Expressive Arts; PSHE)

- Ask pairs to copy each other's movements as they perform fun dance moves. (If it is sunny, go outside so the children can dance with each other's shadows.)
- Afterwards, ask groups to move together to become one shape or moving object (for example, a cube or train).

Small-world friendships (Communication and Language; PSHE)

- Encourage the children to act out friendship scenarios using small-world figures and in the home corner.

My favourite toy (Communication and Language; PSHE)

- Ask the children to draw pictures of their favourite toys and present them to the class in a 'show and tell' session. Encourage children to write their toys' names by their pictures and create a class display.

SEQUENCE ASSESSMENT

Communication and Language

- Does the child listen to the story with increasing attention and recall?
- Does the child anticipate key events in the story?
- Does the child listen and respond to ideas expressed by others in conversation or discussion?
- Does the child use talk to organise, sequence and clarify thinking and ideas about the story?
- Does the child show evidence of extending their vocabulary?
- Does the child explore the story in their play: Mog playing, being upset, friendship and care of Mog, and so on?

Reading

- Is the child aware of how the story is structured?
- Can the child predict how the story might end?
- Can the child describe the main story setting, events and the characters of Mog and the children?
- Can the child hear and say the initial sound in a CVC word or name?
- Can the child segment the sounds in simple CVC words and blend them together?

Writing

- Can the child segment sounds for CVC words relating to the story and write them down?
- Can the child recognise initial sounds for letters in CVC words?
- Can the child write and verbally compose simple sentences using a range of CVC words and their spelling patterns?

Review of the Big Picture

At the end of this sequence, discuss with the children what they liked about the story 'Mog and Bunny'. Ask: *Which section or words did you like? What have you learnt about family and friendship? What new words have you learnt to read and write?*

Encourage each child to show and explain examples of their writing and reading achievements, and any cross-curricular activities they enjoyed.

Use the 'Pupil observation chart' to record each child's responses and attainments.

SEQUENCE 4 Colours: Colours Around Us

TERM 1 (AUTUMN) 2nd half term

Main Topic:	Colours
Subtopic:	Colours Around Us
Text Type:	Poem
Main Source Text:	'Painting' by Irene Rawnsley, from *Time For a Rhyme* edited by Fiona Waters (ISBN 978-1-858-81695-1)
Extra Source Texts:	*Colour Me Happy!* by Shen Roddie (ISBN 978-1-405-00909-6); *Red Rockets and Rainbow Jelly* by Sue Heap (ISBN 978-0-140-56785-4) *Sharing A Shell* by Julia Donaldson (ISBN 978-1-405-02048-0)
Approximate Duration:	Two weeks

Big Picture

During this sequence, children will listen to the poem 'Painting' and discuss its structure, imagery and vocabulary as a group. They will also have the opportunity to join in with the poem, using images for support.

A range of literacy and cross-curricular activities will give the children opportunity to explore colour in nature and their everyday lives.

Phonics Focuses

The children practise hearing and saying sounds for letters, and segmenting and blending sounds in CVC and simple CVCC words for reading and writing. They are also introduced to the grapheme/phoneme correspondences of 'y', 'w', 'j', 'v', 'x', 'qu', 'z' and 'zz'.
Learning Outcomes: See 'Learning Outcomes' Chart, on pages xi–xiv.
Key Vocabulary: painting, yellow, green, blue, red, golden, rushes, iceberg, blazing

Home Links

Encourage children to:
- create drawings or paintings in colour
- look at colours used around their home
- think about the colours used for specific events and purposes
- ask their family members what their favourite colours are and why.

Resources Required

Workbook Pages: 4–11, 17, 29–30

Resource Sheets 4.1–4.2: My Favourite Colour; x, qu and zz Cards

General Resources:

- Red, yellow, green and blue card or material (for story-telling)
- Craft paper
- Red, yellow, green and blue paint
- Paint brushes
- Coloured pens, pencils or crayons
- Coloured tissue paper
- Stiff cardboard
- Red, yellow, green and blue stickers
- Various coloured objects (for example, a red hat, blue sock, yellow toy car and green ruler)
- Coloured images from newspapers or magazines
- Craft materials (for example, pipe cleaners, textiles, macaroni, glitter, wool)

Background Knowledge

Explain to the children that:
- in the poem, 'Painting', the poet, Irene Rawnsley uses the four primary colours, yellow, green, blue and red to show how colour is all around us whether it be in nature, in objects or creatures. Each verse focuses on a different person who states what their favourite colour is and how they are painting images using that colour.

NB: If there are colour-blind children in your class, work with them to appreciate what their understanding of colour is. Give them freedom to respond to the colours they can see, and ensure that the other children appreciate the difference in what they experience.

Performance Ideas and Storytelling Suggestions

- ★ Read through the poem out loud to yourself before performing it to the class, to help you decide where you could add emphasis and intonation to key words or lines (for example, on the first two repetitive lines of each verse, and/or on the colour word).

- ★ Point out examples of the colour being discussed in each verse, so the children can relate to the focus colour.

- ★ Show the four colour cards to the children at the start of each verse so that the children can relate to the focus colour.

Sequence Structure

This chart offers suggestions on the order and timings of exploring the story over a two-week period. However, please feel free to adapt the sessions to your own planning and suitable timings for your whole class or set groups.

Exploring the Poem

Tip: If possible, aim to perform the poem to or with the children regularly over the two-week period, or before any related activity, so that the children get to know the poem and its meaning well.

WEEK 1 (PHASE 1)	WEEKS 1–2 (PHASE 2)	WEEK 2 (PHASE 3)
Introduction to the poem	**Getting to know the poem**	**Performing the poem**
All sections could be done in one session or split over two or three sessions.	Aim to hold one or two sessions on getting to know the poem, each retelling the poem and then including your own choice of activities.	These sessions could be rehearsed and performed at different times across the week.
1. **What do we know?** (15–20 minutes) 2. **Let's listen and talk** (approx. 30 minutes) **Extra consolidation activity:** • Painting the poem (30–45 minutes)	3. **Let's get to know the poem** (10–15 minutes) **'Structure focus' activities:** • Sequencing verses (10–15 minutes) • The odd one out (10–15 minutes) **'Vocabulary focus' activity:** • 'I'm painting like…' (approx. 20 minutes) **'Phonics focus' activity:** • Rhyming words (10–15 minutes)	4. **Let's put on a performance** (20–30 minutes)

Literacy Activities

READING	WRITING	PHONICS WORK
• Colour hunt! • Painting labels	• Our favourite colours • My favourite colour • I can see a…	• Getting to know 'qu' 'x' and 'zz' • Missing letters

Cross-curricular Activities

Adult-led activities:
- Colour corners (Communication and Language; Physical Development)
- Colour trails (Understanding the World; Communication and Language)
- Stained-glass shapes (Expressive Arts)
- Graphing favourite colours (Mathematics)

Child-led activities:
- Messy colours! (Expressive Arts)
- Colour collages (Communication and Language; Understanding the World; Expressive Arts)
- Colour of the day (Communication and Language; Understanding the World)
- Holiday colours (Expressive Arts)

Sequence Assessment

- Communication and Language
- Reading
- Writing
- Review of the Big Picture

EXPLORING THE POEM

PHASE 1: Introduction to the poem

Session 1: What do we know?

Give prompts and open questions to assess the children's current knowledge of colours and where they can find them in the world around us.

Discuss the **Background Knowledge** given above. Then use red, yellow, green and blue paint on craft paper to lead the discussion.

- Select one colour and dip your paint brush into it.
- Ask the children what the colour is called.
- Asking for children's suggestions, paint one thing that is that colour (for example, an apple, the sun, a leaf, the sea).

- Repeat these steps for each colour. (**NB:** Keep your painting for use in later sessions.)
- Discuss the concept of favourite colours, and choose one of the four colours as your favourite. Explain why you like it.
- Ask talk partners to discuss what their favourite colours are, and why they like them.

Explain to the children that they are going to explore more about colours all around us and their favourite colours.

Session 2: Let's listen and talk

Remind the children briefly of their discussion about colour and explain that they are going to listen to a poem about four people who are painting pictures using their favourite colours.

Show the **Storyteller** video for 'Painting' on **Connect**, or read or perform it to the children. If you are performing the poem, use the poem text on **Connect** for hints and directions, and include images if required (see also the **Performance Ideas and Storytelling Suggestions** above).

After the reading, check that the children understand any new or difficult words (see **Key Vocabulary** above).

Ask questions to check the children's understanding of the poem. These can be open to group discussion

or children can pair with talk partners before reporting back to the group. For example:

- *What is being painted with the yellow paint?*
- *What else is yellow?*
- *Why is the painter using green for the woods?*
- *Where are the sailing ships and fish?*
- *What is an iceberg?*
- *Why do you think the twigs and branches are red?*
- *Which coloured painting do think you'd like most? Why?*

Finally, ask the children to close their eyes and imagine the pictures for each verse as you say the poem one more time.

Extra consolidation activity

Painting the poem

- Read through each verse of the poem again carefully, and make four lists of what images are described in each verse, using images if needed.
- Ask the children to choose their favourite verse, and form groups based on this choice.
- Providing paints, paint brushes and craft paper, ask the groups to paint their favourite verse in the correct colour. Encourage children to show how they personally see the picture described in the verse.
- Ask the children to hold up their finished pictures for the relevant verse as you retell the poem again.

EXPLORING THE POEM

PHASE 2: Getting to know the poem

Session 3: Let's get to know the poem 👥 👥

Show the children your coloured painting again, and remind them of the poem. Ask them what they remember about it. Retell the poem using the **Storyteller** video on **Connect**, or perform it again to the class. Then retell the poem again, asking the children to join in with actions and the repeated words of each verse.

After the second retelling, choose focus activities to explore the poem in more depth.

'Structure focus' activities

Sequencing verses 👥 👥

- Hold up cards or paint to represent the colours blue, green, red and yellow (in that order).
- Explain that the colours for the poem have got mixed up and ask the children to help you put them back into the correct order.

Differentiation: If children struggle to remember the poem's order, use action clues to help them (for example, miming a bird, tall tree, fish and then flames).

The odd one out 👥 👥

- Display the interactive activity 'Odd Colour Out'.
- Point to each picture frame and the colour name above it.
- Look at the three objects inside each frame.
- Explain that one of the objects in each frame is not in the right place, and is the 'odd one out'.
- Look again at each object and ask the children to decide which is the 'odd one out'.
- When the selection has been made, put a cross by the object and discuss why it was chosen.

'Vocabulary focus' activity

'I'm painting like… ' 👥 👥

- Ask the children to sit in a circle.
- Read out the first two lines of each verse.
- Ask the children which parts of the verses are the same. (The repeated words are '… is my favourite colour; I'm painting like… '.)
- Explain that you will re-read these lines for each colour, and that you'd like the children to think of new items of the correct colours to add to the poem.
- Ask each child, in turn, to complete your sentence, and say, 'Yellow is my favourite colour; I'm painting like… '.
- Repeat this step, using the colours from the other verses: green, blue and red.

'Phonics focus' activity

Rhyming words 👥 👥

- Point out that some words in the poem rhyme: they end with the same sound.
- Read the first verse with emphasis on the rhyming words, 'sun' and 'done'.
- Ask the children to tell you which two words rhyme.
- Ask the class or groups to look out for the other rhyming pairs in other verses as you read out the poem again.

Differentiation: Encourage more confident readers to use the spelling patterns for clues about rhymes.

EXPLORING THE POEM

PHASE 3: Performing the poem

Session 4: Let's put on a performance 👥 👥

Over the week, encourage the children to explore the poem through role-play by asking them to act out scenes for the things painted in the poem (for example, birds and people enjoying the sun; the grass, rushes, trees and river; fish, people sailing on the sea and polar bears on icebergs; people enjoying a large bonfire). Props or correctly coloured clothing could also be made or brought in for assistance.

During the final session, remind the children of their work so far. Show the poem again using the **Storyteller** video on **Connect**, or retell it with the children from the whiteboard. Then ask the children to work together to create a performance of the poem.

- Allocate four groups of children a verse each.
- Ask each group to prepare a presentation of their lines. This could be:
  - a picture of their verse's painting
  - a mime or hand gestures
  - a role-play scene (as explored over the week).
- Ask the groups to stand in order, and then – as you read out the poem – to give their performances or presentations at the appropriate time.
- Encourage the children to say the colour at the beginnings of their verse, or the rhyming words at the ends of their lines, with you.
- If possible, film the performance for the children to watch and enjoy.

Differentiation: More confident readers may wish to read their lines along with their performances or assist you in reading out the poem.

LITERACY ACTIVITIES

Reading

Colour hunt!

- Create word cards for coloured objects that you have hidden or placed around the room (for example, red hat, blue sock, yellow toy car and green ruler). Each card should display the name of the object (for example, 'hat') written in the relevant colour.
- Lay out the cards and encourage the children to sound, segment and blend the letters to read each word.
- Once a word has been read, check that the children know what colour the object should be.
- Ask them to find the object in the room and bring it back, matching the word card to the object.

Painting labels

- Ask mixed-ability pairs to work on the interactive activity 'Painting Labels', dragging the CVC/CCVC word labels to the correct coloured object on the painting.

Differentiation: Encourage more confident readers to take a lead and peer-support using the sounds they know.

Writing

Our favourite colours

- Ask each child to draw one thing in their favourite colour.
- Write out a caption sentence for each object for each child to copy, and ask them to add their name (for example, '_____ likes red socks.').
- Put all the children's work together and create a class book celebrating the different favourites, ordered by colour.

Differentiation: Encourage more confident writers to write more of their captions themselves.

My favourite colour

- Ask each child to paint their own scene containing any three objects in their favourite colour.
- Then ask the children to say and sound out the three objects' names.
- Write out the colour and the object words, and ask the children to copy them onto Resource Sheet 4.1, to create their own list poems.
- Encourage the children to share their poems, and display them next to their paintings.

Differentiation: Ask more confident writers to spell and write down their colour and objects' names themselves.

I can see a...

- Ask mixed-ability pairs to work on the interactive activity 'I Can See a... ', dragging the letters into order to form the CVC- or CVCC-word picture captions.

Differentiation: Encourage more confident writers to write their own captions for other CVC or CVCC words.

Phonics Work

Getting to know 'qu', 'x' and 'zz'

- Cut out the word cards from Resource Sheet 4.2.
- Show a word containing the letter 'x' to the children.
- Read the word and then sound, segment and blend it. Ask the children to copy you.
- Underline the 'x' and ask the children what sound this letter makes.
- Show the other words containing 'x'.
- Ask the children to sound them out, putting emphasis on the 'x'.
- Repeat these steps for the words containing 'qu'.
- Repeat these steps for the words containing 'zz'.
- Then mix up the cards and lay them out.
- Ask the children to sound out each word, and group the words into sets of the three sounds.

Missing letters

- Ask mixed-ability pairs to work on the interactive activity 'Missing Letters', dragging the missing letters ('y', 'w', 'j', 'v' or 'z') to complete the picture labels.

Differentiation: Ask more confident children to think of alternative object names containing a letter 'y', 'w', 'j', 'v' or 'z', and to create labels for them.

CROSS-CURRICULAR ACTIVITIES

Adult-led activities

Colour corners (Communication and Language; Physical Development)

- Put up a colour sign (red, yellow, green or blue) in each of the four corners of the room.
- Ask the children to stand in the middle of the room.
- Turn your back and call, 'Corners!' The children run to any corner.
- Then call out a colour and turn around: those in that corner are out.
- Repeat, until a winner emerges!

Colour trails (Understanding the World; Communication and Language)

- Create a colour trail around a room or outside for the children to follow, by noticing or placing objects of a certain colour along the route.
- Give each child a prepared tick sheet showing images of the objects to find. (Alternatively, reveal the selected colour and ask children to find the trail, drawing images of the objects they see.)
- If this activity is repeated outside in different seasons, it can highlight nature's changing colours.

Stained-glass windows (Expressive Arts)

- Create simple frames (two per child) by cutting oblong shapes from stiff cardboard.
- Ask the children to make simple 'stained-glass' pictures by sticking strips of coloured tissue across one of the shapes and then sticking the second shape on top to create a frame.
- Hang the pictures in the window.

Graphing favourite colours (Mathematics)

- Ask the children what their favourite of the four colours is.
- Model creating a block graph of this information.
- Ask the children to create their own block graphs using coloured stickers (or a large floor graph using coloured bricks).

Child-led activities

Messy colours! (Expressive Arts)

- Set up a sensory messy play session and ask the children to experiment with mixing primary-colour paints (red, yellow and blue) to see what other colours they can make.

Colour collages (Communication and Language; Understanding the World; Expressive Arts)

- Provide lots of coloured images from newspapers or magazines.
- Give each child a piece of craft paper split into four sections: red, yellow, green and blue.
- Ask the children to select and stick down select examples of things in each colour.

Colour of the day (Communication and Language; Understanding the World)

- Over the two-week period, select a 'colour of the day' on four different days.
- Encourage the children to find examples of that colour during the day.
- Set up the room so that the children get the opportunity to explore and play with colour, for example, colour themed dressing up/home corner, toys, boxes, and so on.

Holiday colours (Expressive Arts)

- Look at colours that are traditionally used during the winter holiday period where you are.
- Create festive decorations in these colours (for example, wreaths, ornaments or garlands).

SEQUENCE ASSESSMENT

Communication and Language
- Does the child listen and respond to discussion about the poem?
- Does the child join in with and recognise repeated refrains in the poem?
- Has the child extended their vocabulary by exploring the meaning and sounds of new words?
- Does the child use talk to organise, sequence and clarify thinking and ideas about the poem and the related poem activities?
- Does the child show evidence of extending their vocabulary?

Reading
- Can the child recognise rhythm in the poem's verses?
- Can the child anticipate key words and rhymes in the poem?
- Can the child hear the initial sounds for words?
- Can the child segment and blend sounds in CVC/CVCC words?
- Can the child recognise the sounds for 'w', 'j', 'y', 'x', 'qu' and 'zz'?

Writing
- Can the child sound out and write their names?
- Can the child write simple labels after an aural prompt?
- Can the child segment and blend sounds in CVC/CVCC words?
- Can the child use some clearly identifiable letters to communicate meaning, representing some sounds correctly and in sequence?
- Can the child begin to write labels and words for captions?

Review of the Big Picture
At the end of this sequence, discuss with the children what they liked about the poem 'Painting'. Ask: *What is your favourite colour? Which verse did you like most? Why? What objects did it describe? Which words were repeated at the beginning of each verse?*

Encourage each child to show and explain examples of their writing and reading achievements, and any cross-curricular activities they enjoyed.

Use the 'Pupil observation chart' to record each child's responses and attainment.

SEQUENCE 5 Colours: Rainbows

TERM 1 (AUTUMN): 2nd half term

Main Topic:	Colours
Subtopic:	Rainbows
Text Type:	Story
Main Source Text:	*Elmer and the Rainbow* by David McKee (ISBN 978-1-842-70716-6)
Extra Source Text:	*The Rainbow Fish* by Marcus Pfizer (ISBN: 978-1-558-58536-2)
Approximate Duration:	Two weeks

Big Picture

During this sequence, children will listen to 'Elmer and the Rainbow' and discuss its messages, characters, events and vocabulary as a group. They will also have the opportunity to explore the characters and events through role-play.

A range of literacy and cross-curricular activities will give the children opportunity to explore rainbows and their colours in more depth.

Phonics Focuses

The children practise hearing and saying sounds for letters, and segmenting and blending sounds in CVC and simple CVCC words for reading and writing. They also rehearse hearing and counting syllables in words.

Learning Outcomes: See 'Learning Outcomes' Chart, on pages xi–xiv.

Key Vocabulary: rainbow, patchwork, colourless, pale, gradually

Home Links

Encourage children to:
- look out for rainbows in the sky, in artwork and in patterns
- look out for rainbow colours in other contexts.

Resources Required

Workbook Pages: 6–12, 20

Resource Sheets 5.1–5.3: Elmer's Rainbow Hunt; Rainbow Word Board; Rainbow Word Cards

General Resources:

- An image or video of a rainbow
- Craft paper
- Crayons, coloured pens and paint in rainbow colours
- String
- Sticky tape
- A4 card, folded to create blank greetings cards
- Craft materials (e.g. paints, glue, tissue paper, pipe cleaners, magazine pictures, wool)
- A glass prism
- A CD
- A tube of bubbles
- A water spray
- Rainbow-coloured strips of crepe paper, material or ribbon
- Hair ties
- Rainbow-coloured beads
- Messy rainbow-coloured materials: cooked spaghetti, modelling dough, jelly, sand or rice

Background Knowledge

Explain to the children that:
- rainbows appear in the sky when there is both sunlight and moisture (usually rain)
- in real life, rainbows are made of light and do not touch the ground (so you can never find the 'start' or 'end' of a rainbow).

NB: If there are colour-blind children in your class, work with them to appreciate what their understanding of colour is. Give them freedom to respond to the colours they can see, and ensure that the other children appreciate the difference in what they experience.

Performance Ideas and Storytelling Suggestions

- ★ Read through the story out loud to yourself before reading it to the class, to help you decide where you could add emphasis and intonation to key words or lines (for example, by creating voices for the different characters, and/or looking at the speech verbs as guides for expression).

- ★ Pause at various points in the story, to ask questions that will encourage the children to make story predictions (for example, *How could the monkeys help Elmer?* or *What do you think might have happened to Elmer when he comes out of the waterfall?*

Sequence Structure

This chart offers suggestions on the order and timings of exploring the story over a two-week period. However, please feel free to adapt the sessions to your own planning and suitable timings for your whole class or set groups.

Exploring the Story

Tip: If possible, aim to read or show the story to the children regularly over the two-week period, or before any related activity, so that the children get to know the story and its messages well.

WEEK 1 (PHASE 1)	WEEKS 1–2 (PHASE 2)	WEEKS 1–2 (PHASE 3)
Introduction to the story	**Getting to know the story**	**Performing the story**
All sections could be done in one session or split over two or three sessions.	Aim to hold one or two sessions on getting to know the story, each retelling the story and then including your own choice of activities.	Aim to hold one or two sessions at different times across the two-week period.
1. **What do we know?** (approx. 20 minutes) 2. **Let's listen and talk** (approx. 20 minutes) **Extra consolidation activity:** ● Elmer's happiness patchwork (approx. 30 minutes)	3. **Let's get to know the story** (10–15 minutes) **'Structure focus' activities:** ● Who helps Elmer? (approx. 20 minutes) ● Sequencing Elmer's rainbow hunt (30–40 minutes) **'Vocabulary focus' activity:** ● Making a new word (approx. 15 minutes) **'Phonics focus' activity:** ● Animal syllables (approx. 15 minutes)	4. **Let's put on a performance** (20–30 minutes)

Literacy Activities

READING	WRITING	PHONICS WORK
● Rainbow-colour initials ● Rainbow books ● Elmer's gifts	● Thank-you cards ● Patchwork words	● Patchwork rhyming words

Cross-curricular Activities

Adult-led activities:
● Rainbow investigations (Communication and Language; Understanding the World)
● Rainbow dance and music (Expressive Arts)
● Modelling 'Elmer and the Rainbow' (Expressive Arts)

Child-led activities:
● Rainbow beads (Mathematics; Expressive Arts)
● Rainbow mess! (Expressive Arts)
● Rainbow pictures (Expressive Arts)
● Sorting rainbow colours (Mathematics)

Sequence Assessment

● Communication and Language
● Reading
● Writing
● Review of the Big Picture

EXPLORING THE STORY

PHASE 1: Introduction to the story

Session 1: What do we know?

Show the children a picture or video of a rainbow. Give prompts and ask open questions to assess their current knowledge about rainbows. For example:

- *What is this called?*
- *Who has seen a rainbow before? Where?*
- *Use an arm and hand to show me the shape of a rainbow.*
- *Why do you think this is called a rainbow?*

- *What colours can you see in the rainbow?* (red, orange, yellow, green, blue, purple and possibly light purple or pink)
- *What do you like about rainbows?*
- *How would you feel if you saw a rainbow without any colours in it?*

Discuss the **Background Knowledge** given above. Then explain that the children are going to listen to a story about an elephant called Elmer, who tried to mend a rainbow that has lost its colours.

Session 2: Let's listen and talk

Remind the children briefly of their discussion about rainbows and explain that they are going to listen to a story about an elephant called Elmer and a rainbow without any colours. Ask the children how they think Elmer will help the rainbow.

Show the **Storyteller** video for 'Elmer and the Rainbow' on **Connect**, or read the story yourself (see the **Performance Ideas and Storytelling Suggestions** above).

After the reading, check that the children understand any new or difficult words (see **Key Vocabulary** above).

Ask questions to check the children's understanding of the story. These can be open to group discussion or children can pair with talk partners before reporting back to the group. For example:

- *How is Elmer different to the other elephants?*
- *What does Elmer need to find, in order to help the rainbow?*

- *What do you think might happen to Elmer if he gives his colours to the rainbow?*
- *Where does Elmer find the rainbow?*
- *How does he give his colours to the rainbow?*
- *Why does Elmer still have his colours?*
- *How do the animals feel at the end of the story?*

Finally, look back at the illustrations and point out all the different colours in the story. Ask the children to share which illustrations they like most, and what colours and shapes they can see.

Extra consolidation activity

Elmer's happiness patchwork

- Remind the children of what Elmer said at the end of the story about giving happiness or love or his colours.
- Discuss the fact that people can get happiness back by giving it to others.
- Ask children to give examples of ways they have recently made someone happy.
- Draw patchwork-type squares on the board, one for each child and yourself.
- In one of the squares, model writing a way you could give happiness (for example, 'Patting my cat').
- Ask the children to suggest ways they could give happiness, and write their ideas into the patchwork squares.
- Afterwards, read through all their suggestions.
- Over the two weeks that this sequence runs, praise the children for instances of giving happiness.

Differentiation: Encourage more confident children to create a patchwork by drawing their example, with a short caption, onto a piece of paper. Join all the sheets together to form the patchwork.

EXPLORING THE STORY

PHASE 2: Getting to know the story

Session 3: Let's get to know the story 👥 👥

Show the children the rainbow again, and remind them of the story. Ask them what they remember about it. Retell the story using the **Storyteller** video on **Connect**, or read the story again yourself.

After the retelling, choose focus activities to explore the story in more depth.

'Structure focus' activities

Who helps Elmer? 👥 👥

- Display the interactive activity 'Who Helps Elmer?'.
- Ask the children to look at the range of different animals on the screen.
- Then look at each animal in turn and ask the children if it appeared in the story, placing a tick or a cross by each.
- Once the correct animals have been selected, discuss how they helped Elmer in the story.

Sequencing Elmer's rainbow hunt 👥 👥

- Cut out the images from Resource Sheet 5.1 and show them in a mixed-up order.
- Ask the children to help you to sort the images into the correct order by retelling the story in their own words.
- Then give out sets of the pictures to small mixed-ability groups and ask them to work together to order the images and colour them in.
- Attach string to one set of images and hang it up for future reference.

'Vocabulary focus' activity

Making a new word 👥 👥

- Display the interactive activity 'Making a New Word'.
- Explain that new words can sometimes be formed when two other words are joined together.
- Point to the images of rain and the bow, and then click on the box by the two images to reveal the answer. Say the new word together.
- Continue, prompting the children to name the images and recognise the new (compound) words.

Differentiation: Encourage more confident children to take a lead in generating other simple compound words.

'Phonics focus' activity

Animal syllables 👥 👥

- Display an image of Elmer from **Connect**.
- Say 'Elmer' loudly, and clap the two syllables as you say it. Ask the children to copy you.
- Ask them to help you with a clapping game using the names of animals in the story.
- Start with one-syllable animal names (for example, 'bird', 'fish') and then use two-syllable names (for example, 'lion', 'tiger', 'rabbit', 'monkey'), and finally choose three-syllable names (for example, 'crocodile', 'elephant').
- Say the name each time, with a clap or claps to show the number of syllables, and then ask the children to follow.

Differentiation: You could progress to using other words in the story for syllable rhythms (for example, 'rain', 'rainbow', 'waterfall').

EXPLORING THE STORY

PHASE 3: Performing the story

Session 4: Let's put on a performance

Over the two weeks, encourage the children to explore the story through role-play. For example:

- Ask the children to role-play discovering that something else in their experience has changed and needs to be mended (for example, the sky changing colour or the seasons being mixed up). Ask children how they might react and what they could do to try and fix the problem.

- Have a 'movement and mime' session, asking the children to explore how each of the animals in the story (elephants, birds, lions, tigers, rabbits, giraffes, monkeys, fish and crocodiles) would move and act. Once they have had a chance to explore each animal, allocate them into animal groups and ask them to think of ways their animal may be able to look for the end of the rainbow.

During the final session, remind the children of their work so far. Show the story again using the **Storyteller** video on **Connect**, or retell it with the children from the whiteboard. Then ask the children to work together to act out the story.

- Allocate groups of children to be the different animal characters using their animal role-play skills.

- Discuss and establish a sequence trail around the room, ending with the river and waterfall, and set the groups at different points of the trail in the correct order (birds, lions, tigers, rabbits, giraffes, elephants, monkeys, fish and crocodiles).

- Give each group a simple, repetitive sentence (for example, 'We must find the rainbow and give it colours').

- Move around the trail as Elmer, reading the story as you walk, and encourage the children to respond in character.

- Ensure that all groups come together to celebrate at the end of the story.

LITERACY ACTIVITIES

Reading

Rainbow-colour initials

- Give small groups or pairs a copy of Resource Sheet 5.2 and a set of the word cards, cut out from Resource Sheet 5.3.
- Point to the first initial letter on Resource Sheet 5.2, 'r', and sound this out.
- Ask the children to work out what colour word starts with 'r', and assist them if necessary.
- Repeat this for each initial letter, 'o' for 'orange', 'y' for 'yellow', 'g' for 'green', 'b' for 'blue' and 'p' for 'purple'.
- Mix up and lay out the word cards.
- Ask the children to sound out the words' initial letters.
- Finally, ask them to place the cards onto the correct rainbow section of Resource Sheet 5.2.

Differentiation: More confident readers could create more word cards using the same initial-letter sounds.

Rainbow books

- Ask pairs to find fun and interesting books about rainbows.
- Create a rainbow-themed story section to allow the children to share their books.

Elmer's gifts

- Ask mixed-ability pairs to work on the interactive activity 'Elmer's Gifts', listening to and sounding out the labels, and matching them with their objects.

Differentiation: More confident children could try and match more objects with labels you provide, using longer CVCC or CCVC words, or words containing digraphs (for example, 'ai').

Writing

Thank-you cards

- Remind the children how kind Elmer was being when he went to give the rainbow his colours, and suggest that the children write a thank-you card from one of the other animal characters.
- Ask the children to suggest what they could say in their cards (for example, 'Thank you, Elmer' and 'You are kind').
- Write out the message(s) for the children to copy onto their cards.
- Encourage each child to write the animal's name – or their name – on their card too, and then to decorate it.

Differentiation: Write out only part of the message for more confident readers to complete on their cards.

Patchwork words

- Ask mixed-ability pairs to work on the interactive activity 'Patchwork Words', dragging the missing letters into the words on the patchwork squares.

Phonics Work

Patchwork rhyming words

- Ask mixed-ability pairs to work on the interactive activity 'Elmer's Rhyming Words', matching the six pairs of rhyming words.

Differentiation: More confident children could think of alternative words that rhyme with the words shown in the activity. Encourage them to write these out on cards for use in a pairs game.

CROSS-CURRICULAR ACTIVITIES

Adult-led activities

Rainbow investigations (Communication and Language; Understanding the World)

- With the children, investigate different ways that a rainbow can appear. For example:
  - through a glass prism
  - on a CD
  - in bubbles
  - when water mist is sprayed in the sunshine.

Rainbow dance and music (Expressive Arts)

- Ask the children to create rainbow-coloured dance streamers using rainbow-coloured strips of crepe paper, material or ribbon attached to hair ties that can be worn as wrist-bands.
- Have a weather dance and music session, asking the children to pretend to be rain, thunder and lightning, and then the sun, before the rainbows appear.

Modelling 'Elmer and the Rainbow' (Expressive Arts)

- Allocate different parts of the story's scenery to different groups (for example, the grey and coloured rainbows, the characters, and bushes, trees and the river).
- Ask the groups to create a 3D model or wall display of this part of the story, using all available craft materials.
- Assemble the scene, and use this to assist the children in independently retelling the story.

Child-led activities

Rainbow beads (Mathematics; Expressive Arts)

- Give the children an assortment of rainbow-coloured beads and ask them to sort them into their colours.
- Ask them to thread the beads onto a string to create a rainbow pattern.
- Afterwards, encourage them to create new bead patterns of their own.
- The bead strings could then become bracelets or bookmarks.

Rainbow mess! (Expressive Arts)

- Set up a sensory messy play session using unusual (and messy!) rainbow-coloured materials such as cooked spaghetti, modelling dough, jelly, or sand or rice.
- Ask the children to play with these materials to make rainbows and other patterns.

Rainbow pictures (Expressive Arts)

- Ask the children to make their own rainbow pictures using a range of craft materials, for example, by gluing scrunched-up tissue paper, pipe cleaners, half paper plates, pictures from magazines or coloured sand.

Sorting rainbow colours (Mathematics)

- Ask the children to sort their various craft or other classroom materials by colour.
- Then ask them to count and organise the materials in each set.

SEQUENCE ASSESSMENT

Communication and Language
- Does the child listen to the story with increasing attention and recall?
- Does the child anticipate key events in the story?
- Does the child listen and respond to ideas expressed by others in conversation or discussion?
- Does the child use talk to organise, sequence and clarify thinking and ideas about the story?
- Does the child show evidence of extending their vocabulary?
- Does the child introduce and explore the story in their play?

Reading
- Is the child aware of how the story is structured?
- Can the child predict how the story might end?
- Can the child describe the main story setting, events and main characters?
- Does the child show interest in the story's illustrations?
- Can the child hear and say the initial sounds in words?
- Can the child segment the sounds in simple words and blend them together?
- Does the child know what letters represent some sounds?

Writing
- Can the child segment and blend the sounds for words and write them down?
- Can the child recognise initial sounds for letters in words?
- Can the child link sounds to letters and names?
- Can the child write their own name and simple labels and captions?

Review of the Big Picture
At the end of this sequence, discuss with the children what they liked about 'Elmer and the Rainbow'. Ask: *Which section did you like most, and why? Which is your favourite character? What have you learnt from the story? Why do you think Elmer didn't lose his colours?*

Encourage each child to show and explain examples of their writing and reading achievements, and any cross-curricular activities about rainbows and the story that they enjoyed.

Use the 'Pupil observation chart' to record each child's responses and attainment.

SEQUENCE 6 Colours: Festival Colours

TERM 1 (AUTUMN): 2nd half term

Main Topic:	Colours
Subtopic:	Festival Colours
Text Type:	Story
Main Source Text:	*A Story of Diwali: The Festival of Light* by Pippa Howard (ISBN 978-0-957-44810-4)
Approximate Duration:	Two weeks

Big Picture

During this sequence, children will listen to 'A Story of Diwali' and discuss its messages, characters, events and vocabulary as a group. They will also have the opportunity to explore the characters and events through role-play.

Through a range of supportive activities, the children will have the opportunity to investigate the traditions and festivities of the Diwali festival in more depth.

Phonics Focuses

The children will learn to recognise tricky and regular words, practise hearing and saying initial-letter sounds, and segment and blend sounds in CVC and simple CVCC words.

Learning Outcomes: See 'Learning Outcomes' Chart, on pages xi–xiv.

Key Vocabulary: banish, cunning, demons, cautiously, transform, distraught, diva, Diwali

Home Links

Encourage children to:
- find out where India is
- make shapes and Rangoli patterns
- find out more about Diwali (for example, fireworks, traditional foods and more stories).

Resources Required

Workbook Pages: 4–6, 13–16
Resource Sheets 6.1–6.3: Rangoli Patterns; Rama and Sita Story Map 1–2

General Resources:
- A diva lamp
- Craft paper
- Paper plates
- Black card
- Self-hardening clay
- Recorded Diwali music, or internet access and speakers
- Simple percussion instruments such as tambourines
- Wooden lollipop sticks
- Craft materials (e.g. coloured sand, glitter, paint, glue, tape, pens, pipe cleaners, coloured tissue paper, cloth, dried pasta, wool)
- A4 card, folded to create blank greetings cards

Background Knowledge

Explain to the children that:
- the festival of Diwali is celebrated by Hindus all over the world
- Hinduism is a religion with 1 billion followers: 15% of the global population. The majority of Hindus reside in India, Nepal, Mauritius and Bali (in Indonesia)
- Diwali is held over five days in October or November
- in Sanskrit, 'diwali' means 'a row of lamps' It celebrates Lakshmi, the Hindu goddess of goodness and wealth
- during the festival, families hope to welcome Lakshmi into to their homes by filling them with light and colour. They light clay lamps called 'divas', and create colourful patterns (called Rangoli patterns) from coloured rice flour
- families also have parties, give each other gifts and cards, eat special foods, and tell the story of Rama and Sita.

NB: If there are colour-blind children in your class, work with them to appreciate what their understanding of colour is. Give them freedom to respond to the colours they can see, and ensure that the other children appreciate the difference in what they experience.

Performance Ideas and Storytelling Suggestions

- ★ Read through the story out loud to yourself before reading it to the class, to help you decide where you could add emphasis and intonation to key words or lines (for example, to highlight surprise and action).
- ★ Speak slowly and use physical movements to help the children understand what certain words mean (for example, 'transform', 'banish', 'cautiously', 'distraught').
- ★ Use music or musical beats to build up the suspense or excitement of events, as well as the ending celebration. (Diwali music playlists can be found for free online: try searching for 'Diwali Songs' on a video-hosting website.)

Sequence Structure

This chart offers suggestions on the order and timings of exploring the story over a two-week period. However, please feel free to adapt the sessions to your own planning and suitable timings for your whole class or set groups.

Exploring the Story

Tip: If possible, aim to read or show the story to the children regularly over the two-week period, or before any related activity, so that the children get to know the story and its messages well.

WEEK 1 (PHASE 1)	WEEKS 1–2 (PHASE 2)	WEEKS 1–2 (PHASE 3)
Introduction to the story	**Getting to know the story**	**Performing the story**
All sections could be done in one session or split over two or three sessions.	Aim to hold one or two sessions on getting to know the story, each retelling the story and then including your own choice of activities.	Aim to hold one or two sessions at different times across the two-week period.
1. **What do we know?** (20–30 minutes) 2. **Let's listen and talk** (approx. 30 minutes) **Extra consolidation activity:** • Character emotion masks (approx. 30 minutes) • Diwali friendship mobiles (approx. 30 minutes)	3. **Let's get to know the story** (10–15 minutes) **'Structure focus' activity:** • Rama and Sita story map (approx. 20 minutes) **'Vocabulary focus' activity:** • Getting to know the characters (approx. 20 minutes) **'Phonics focus' activity:** • Word lamp trail (approx. 15 minutes)	4. **Let's put on a performance** (20–30 minutes)

Literacy Activities

READING	WRITING	PHONICS WORK
• Indian animal initials • Word bridges	• Diwali cards • Rangoli letter writing • What is the Diwali gift?	• CVC rescue bridges • Find the letters

Cross-curricular Activities

Adult-led activities:
- Rangoli patterns (Expressive Arts; Understanding the World)
- Rangoli shapes (Mathematics; Expressive Arts)
- Story shadows (Communication and Language; Expressive Arts)
- Diwali sweets (Understanding the World)

Child-led activities:
- Diva lamps (Expressive Arts; Understanding the World)
- Diwali gifts (Expressive Arts; Understanding the World)
- Diwali trails (Physical Development; Communication and Language)

Sequence Assessment

- Communication and Language
- Reading
- Writing
- Review of the Big Picture

EXPLORING THE STORY

PHASE 1: Introduction to the story

Session 1: What do we know?

Show the children a diva lamp and ask them if they know what it is.

(If children in your class celebrate Diwali, encourage them to help you lead the following discussion.)

Explain that lamps called 'divas' are used every year as part of the Hindu religious festival of Diwali. Encourage the children to say 'Diwali'. Write the word out, and point out that the 'w' is said as a 'v'. Check the children understand the concepts of religion and festivals, using other examples if necessary.

Discuss the **Background Knowledge** given above, explaining what the festival of Diwali means, and how it is celebrated by Hindu children all over the world. Show the images from Resource Sheet 6.1 and, if you have internet access available, show further images to help illustrate this information (for example, fireworks, more diva maps, a map showing India).

Then explain to the children that they are going to learn and explore more about Diwali, including hearing the special story of Rama and Sita.

Session 2: Let's listen and talk

Show the diva lamp to the children again and explain that they are going to listen to the special Diwali story of Rama and Sita.

Show the **Storyteller** video for 'A Story of Diwali' on **Connect**, or read the story yourself (see the **Performance Ideas and Storytelling Suggestions** above).

After the reading, check that the children understand any new or difficult words (see **Key Vocabulary** above).

Ask questions to check the children's understanding of the story. These can be open to group discussion or children can pair with talk partners before reporting back to the group. For example:

- *Who were Rama and Sita?*

- *Where did the stepmother send Rama?*
- *Why did Sita and Lakshman go with Rama?*
- *What did Lakshman make to keep Sita safe?*
- *How was Sita tricked?*
- *Who took Sita?*
- *What did King Hanuman and his monkeys build?*
- *What did people do to help Rama and Sita find their way home?*
- *How do people remember the story of Rama and Sita?*

Finally, look at and discuss all the examples of friendship in the story. Ask the children to think about and discuss what they think it means to be a good friend.

Extra consolidation activity

Character emotion masks

- Hand out a paper plate and lollipop stick to each child, and make craft materials available.
- Assist the children in sticking the sticks to the plates, so they can be held up as face masks.
- Ask each child to draw a happy face on one side of their mask and a sad face on the other, and then to decorate their masks colourfully, using Rangoli patterns as inspiration (see Resource Sheet 6.1).
- Retell the story, and ask the children to hold up the correct sides of their masks to show when Rama and Sita are happy and sad.
- After the retelling, talk about what made the characters happy or sad each time the plates were turned.

Diwali friendship mobiles

- Ask the children to think of a family member or friend. Ask: *How could you be a good friend to them?* Let them discuss their ideas within the group.
- Give each child a large card circle to draw their person and friendship action in the middle.
- Let them decorate the outside with Rangoli patterns and glitter.
- Use the circles to make friendship mobiles or a friendship Diwali garland across the room.
- You could also attach simple sentences under each circle.

EXPLORING THE STORY

PHASE 2: Getting to know the story

Session 3: Let's get to know the story 👥 👥

Show the children the lamp again, and remind them of the story. Ask them what they remember about it. Retell the story using the **Storyteller** video on **Connect**, or read the story again yourself.

After the retelling, choose focus activities to explore the story in more depth.

'Structure focus' activity

Rama and Sita story map 👥 👥

- Create a story map using cut out images from Resource Sheets 6.2–6.3. Add your own images to the story map if needed. Use the lamp template on the resource sheet to make lamps for each child.
- Create a display board or felt board to attach the images.
- Encourage the children to help you retell the story and build up a circular story map starting and ending at the palace.
- Let the children colour in their lamps and add them to the lit path.
- Keep the story map displayed to enable the children to look at or retell the story to each other.

'Vocabulary focus' activity

Getting to know the characters 👥 👥

- Display the interactive activity 'Story Characters'.
- Remind the children of the main characters and their names, focusing on Rama, Sita and Ravana.
- Look at the characters' names on the screen. Ask the children to make the sound for each initial letter to help them to guess each name.
- Read out a character's traits and then encourage the children to help you to match the correct descriptions to the correct character's lamp.
- Discuss examples of how the characters showed these traits in the story.

'Phonics focus' activity

Word lamp trail 👥 👥 👥

- Display the interactive activity 'Word Lamp Trail'.
- Click on the first lamp in the trail to reveal the word: 'lamp'. Say the word, modelling segmenting and blending it as the children copy you.
- Follow the trail around, modelling and then asking the children to sound out, segment and blend each word.
- At the end of the trail, put the children into pairs and give each pair a simple CVC/CVCC word to sound, segment and blend.
- After this practice, ask the pairs to share their words with the group or class.

Differentiation: Continue to support less confident children with their segmenting and blending.

EXPLORING THE STORY

PHASE 3: Performing the story

Session 4: Let's put on a performance 👥 👥

Over the two weeks, encourage the children to explore the story through role-play. For example:

- Ask the children to use musical sounds to illustrate different moods and parts of the story. Encourage them to listen to and choose each sound carefully, and then also to use their bodies and facial expressions to show the mood.

- Discuss how the sick old man transformed into Ravana. Ask the children to mime this, concentrating on how they could use their bodies and faces to show each character and then how they could slowly transform from one to another.

During the final session, remind the children of their work so far. Show the story again using the **Storyteller** video on **Connect**, or retell it with the children from the whiteboard. Then ask the children to work together to act out the story.

- Allocate the roles of characters from the story to some children.

- Ask the other children to become forest animals and then members of the monkey army building the bridge (possibly using mats or soft play blocks).

- Read out the story as the children perform their roles.

- At the end of the story, if the children have created their own diva lanterns (see **Cross-curricular Activities**, below), let them use these to lay out a trail for Rama and Sita. Let the children take turns being Rama and Sita, as others become cheering villagers.

LITERACY ACTIVITIES

Reading

Indian animal initials

- Ask mixed-ability pairs to work on the interactive activity 'Indian Animal Initials', adding the missing initial letters to complete the words.

Differentiation: More confident readers could try and clap the syllables for each animal name and count how many syllables are in each one.

Word bridges

- Prepare sets of 'regular' word cards: 'is', 'it', 'in', 'at' and 'and'.
- Prepare sets of 'tricky' word cards: 'no', 'go', 'I', 'the' and 'to'.
- Take on the character of Hanuman, and lay out one set of regular word cards as though you are building the stone bridge across the sea. Encourage the children to sound out each word.
- Then lay out one set of tricky word cards, again as though you are building the stone bridge across the sea. Point out that these words can't be sounded out as easily. Explore which letters sound as expected and which don't.
- When the bridges are built, encourage children to use each word orally, in a simple sentence related to the story.
- Ask pairs to use the sets of cards to play 'Snap' and 'Pairs'.

Differentiation: Combine the regular and tricky word cards for more confident children to sort out into two groups.

Writing

Diwali cards and hangers

- Ask the children to decorate blank cards or long paper wall hangers with their own colourful Diwali pictures and craft-material decorations, using Rangoli patterns as inspiration (see Resource Sheet 6.1).
- Then ask them to copy out 'Happy Diwali' onto their cards, and sign them by writing their names.

Differentiation: More confident writers could add a simple sentence, such as 'I lit a Diwali lamp'.

Rangoli letter writing

- Ask each child to write out the letters of their name on a large sheet of craft paper, and to trace them out with their finger for practice.
- Then ask children to decorate their letters using colourful craft materials to form Rangoli patterns (see Resource Sheet 6.1 for inspiration).

Differentiation: More confident writers may wish to write out and decorate their whole names.

What is the Diwali gift?

- Ask mixed-ability pairs to work on interactive activity 'What is the Diwali Gift?', typing out the words that they see and hear.

Differentiation: Less confident writers may need extra support, or could focus on the letters they are familiar with in each gift word.

Phonics Work

CVC rescue bridges

- Ask mixed-ability pairs to work on the interactive activity 'CVC Rescue Bridges', sorting the words by their vowel sounds.

Differentiation: Encourage more confident children to think of VC spelling patterns to match the words on the last bridge.

Find the letters

- Create letter cards, and hide them around the room.
- Give the children tick-sheets that list the letters to find.
- Once the children have collected and ticked off their letters, ask them to spread them out and to say the sound of each letter.
- Then ask groups to use four of the letters to make the word 'lamp'. Encourage them to sound out, segment and blend the letters as they do this.
- Encourage the groups to make up more words using the letters.

Differentiation: Encourage more confident children to add in more letters to make more words.

CROSS-CURRICULAR ACTIVITIES

Adult-led activities 👥👤

Rangoli patterns (Expressive Arts; Understanding the World)

- Show the children the examples of Rangoli patterns on Resource Sheet 6.1.
- Ask them to experiment with drawing swirls, shapes and patterns for their own Rangoli pictures.
- Provide brightly coloured craft materials for children to use when filling in their patterns.
- Display the Rangoli pictures on the floor for the children to see and enjoy.

Rangoli shapes (Mathematics; Expressive Arts)

- Create a set of simple shape templates in different sizes (for example, circles, squares and triangles).
- Give small groups a set each, making sure the children know what each shape is called.
- Ask the children to sort the shapes into sizes and types.
- Then let them explore and select shapes to create a fun Rangoli pattern.
- Encourage them to stick down or draw around the shapes and then to decorate them.

Differentiation: You may wish to draw a Rangoli shape pattern for less confident children to decorate. More confident children can attempt to make more complex designs.

Story shadows (Communication and Language; Expressive Arts)

- Create basic shadow puppets of the story characters (Rama, Sita, Lakshman, Ravana and Hanuman) and some simple settings (for example, a tree; the palace) using black card and lollipop sticks.
- Ask the children take turns to hold them up as you retell the story with their assistance.

Diwali sweets (Understanding the World)

Make coconut laddoos, a popular Indian sweet that requires no cooking:

- For each group of five children, provide around one can of sweetened condensed milk and a large cup of desiccated coconut.
- Mix the condensed milk and coconut into a firm paste.
- Roll the paste into walnut-sized balls and coat them in extra coconut.

Child-led activities 👥👤 👤👤

Diva lamps (Expressive Arts; Understanding the World)

- Show your diva lamp to the children again.
- Ask the children to use self-hardening clay to mould and make simple diva lamps of their own.
- Once the clay is dry, they should decorate their lamps brightly.

Diwali gifts (Expressive Arts; Understanding the World)

- Ask the children to use their imagination to create a friendship token as a Diwali gift.
- Gift ideas could include simple crafts such as macaroni necklaces, wool bracelets, clay models or paper flowers.

Diwali trails (Physical Development; Communication and Language)

- Ask the children to use classroom or outside objects to create a trail for other children to follow. (They could, for example, draw arrows on paper or form them from sticks.)
- Alternatively, ask children to come up with oral instructions for their partners to follow to complete the trail.

SEQUENCE ASSESSMENT

Communication and Language

- Does the child listen to the story with increasing attention and recall?
- Does the child listen and respond to ideas expressed by others in conversation or discussion?
- Does the child use talk to organise, sequence and clarify thinking and ideas about the story?
- Does the child show evidence of extending their vocabulary?
- Does the child introduce and explore the story in their play?

Reading

- Is the child aware of how the story is structured?
- Can the child describe the main story setting, events and main characters?
- Can the child hear and say the initial sound in CVC words and names?
- Can the child link sounds to different letters?
- Can the child segment the sounds in simple CVC words and blend them together?

Writing

- Can the child give meaning to marks they make as they draw, write and paint?
- Can the child segment sounds for CVC and CVCC words and write them down?
- Can the child recognise initial sounds for letters in CVC words?
- Can the child link sounds to different letters?
- Can the child use clearly identifiable letters to communicate meaning, representing some sounds correctly and in sequence?

Review of the Big Picture

At the end of this sequence, discuss with the children what they liked about 'A Story of Diwali'. Encourage them to retell the story using the storyboard. Ask: *Which part did you like most? Which is your favourite character, and why? What do people do during Diwali to remember Rama and Sita? What have you learnt about Diwali?*

Encourage each child to show and explain examples of their writing and reading achievements, and any cross-curricular activities they enjoyed.

Use the 'Pupil observation chart' to record each child's responses and attainment.

SEQUENCE 7 Food: Apples

TERM 2 (SPRING): 1st half term

Main Topic:	Food
Subtopic:	Apples
Text Type:	Poem
Main Source Text:	'The Apple' by Gillian Floyd, from *A First Poetry Book* edited by Pie Corbett and Gaby Morgan (ISBN 978-0-330-54374-3)
Extra Source Texts:	'Oliver's Fruit Salad' by Vivian French and 'Ten Apples Up On Top' by Dr Seuss, both from *A First Poetry Book* edited by Pie Corbett and Gaby Morgan (ISBN 978-0-330-54374-3)
Approximate Duration:	Two weeks

Big Picture

During this sequence, children will listen to the poem 'The Apple' and discuss its meaning, structure and vocabulary as a group. They will join in with the poem using actions, and will enact it.

The children will become familiar with simple descriptive words relating to apples, write labels identifying parts of an apple, and create a class apple poem.

Through a range of supportive activities, the children will have the opportunity to investigate the differences in apples, grow pips/seeds, create simple recipes and pieces of artwork related to apples, as well as using role-play.

Phonics Focuses

The children will investigate words with the letter sounds 'i-p' and the letter/sound correspondences of the long vowels /ee/ and /oo/.

Learning Outcomes: See 'Learning Outcomes' Chart, on pages xi–xiv.

Key Vocabulary: apple, bite, crunchy, core, pips, seeds, smooth, eventually, light, soil, branches, juicy

Home Links

Encourage children to:
- explore different types of apples when shopping
- try out a simple apple recipe at home
- find and share fiction or non-fiction texts about apples with parents or carers.

Resources Required

Workbook Pages: 4–12, 20–21
Resource Sheet 7.1: How Apples Grow

General Resources:
- Apples
- An apple core with pips/seeds
- Apple pips/seeds (as many as it is possible to collect)
- An open tray of soil
- Images of rain, sun, shoots in soil and apple trees
- A pre-prepared paper or card apple tree with several branches (attached to a display board)
- Craft paper
- Pictures of apples from magazines or newspapers, or printed from a computer
- Paint
- Small-world toys (human figures, lorries, ships)

Background Knowledge

Explain to the children that:
- apple trees can be grown from apple pips/seeds, but that it can take up to six years for them to start producing apples
- when they are mature enough to produce fruit, the trees start to blossom in the spring. The blossom is followed by buds that grow into apples by late summer and early autumn
- there are many varieties of apples. Each type has a distinct taste, texture, size and colour.

Performance Ideas and Storytelling Suggestions

- ★ Read through the poem out loud to yourself before performing it to the class, to help you decide where you could add emphasis and intonation to key words or lines (for example, emphasising 'bite', 'core', 'ground' or 'deep, dark soil').
- ★ When performing the poem, try using physical props (for example, apples, an apple core with pips, a tray of soil to plant pips/seeds, and images of the rain, sun and shoots in soil. You could also mime the actions as you say them (for example, biting an apple or digging in the ground).
- ★ In Phase 2, use hand actions (see 'The Apple' text on **Connect**). Practise and learn these before performing them to the children.

Sequence Structure

This chart offers suggestions on the order and timings of exploring the story over a two-week period. However, please feel free to adapt the sessions to your own planning and suitable timings for your whole class or set groups.

Exploring the Poem

Tip: If possible, aim to perform the poem to or with the children regularly over the two-week period, or before any related activity, so that the children get to know the poem and its meaning well.

WEEK 1 (PHASE 1) Introduction to the poem	WEEKS 1–2 (PHASE 2) Getting to know the poem	WEEK 2 (PHASE 3) Performing the poem
All sections could be done in one session or split over two or three sessions.	Aim to hold one or two sessions on getting to know the poem, each retelling the poem and then including your own choice of activities.	This session could be rehearsed and performed at different times across the week.
1. **What do we know?** (15–20 minutes) 2. **Let's listen and talk** (approx. 30 minutes) **Extra consolidation activity:** • Drawing and describing an apple (approx. 30 minutes)	3. **Let's get to know the poem** (10–15 minutes) **'Structure focus' activities:** • Sequencing different parts of the poem (approx. 10 minutes) • Sequencing how apples grow (10–15 minutes) **'Vocabulary focus' activities:** • Describing apples (15–20 minutes) • Composing a class apple poem (15–20 minutes) **'Phonics focus' activity:** • CVC: Investigating 'p-i-p' (approx. 10 minutes)	4. **Let's put on a performance** (20–30 minutes)

Literacy Activities

READING	WRITING	PHONICS WORK
• Matching tree labels • Exploring and labelling apples • Finding apple information • Finding the missing words	• Finding uses for apples • Making pip letters • Creating apple cards • Giving apples names • Making labels	• CVC phonemes • /ee/ and /oo/

Cross-curricular Activities

Adult-led activities:
• Cooking (PSHE)
• Investigating apples (Understanding the World)
• Planting apple pips/seeds (Understanding the World)
• Apple tasting graphs (Mathematics)

Child-led activities:
• Apple art (Expressive Arts)
• Shopping for apples (Communication and Language; Understanding the World)
• Transporting apples (Communication and Language; Understanding the World)
• Apple counting (Mathematics)

Sequence Assessment

• Communication and Language
• Reading
• Writing
• Review of the Big Picture

EXPLORING THE POEM

PHASE 1: Introduction to the poem

Session 1: What do we know?

Show the children an apple. Give prompts to assess their current knowledge of what an apple is.

For example:

- *What is this?*
- *What is an apple?* (a fruit)
- *Who has eaten an apple before?*
- *Discuss with your talk partner how apples taste and feel.*
- *Where do apples grow? Who has picked an apple off a tree or seen them on trees?* (Show images of apple trees to reinforce the answer.)

- *Where else can we get apples?* (at a shop or stall)
- *Show an apple pip/seed. This is part of an apple. What is it called?* (If children say 'a seed', note that apple seeds are often called pips.)
- *Where do you think apples have pips?*

Discuss the **Background Knowledge** given above. Then explain to the children that they are going to learn about apples and apple pips/seeds and do lots of fun activities about them.

Session 2: Let's listen and talk

Introduce the poem 'The Apple' by holding up an apple and a pip. Highlight that the poem is about an apple and pips. Remind the children briefly of their discussion about apples and pips.

Show the **Storyteller** video for 'The Apple' on **Connect**, or display the poem and read it aloud. If you are performing the poem, use 'The Apple Actions' on **Connect** for hints and directions, and include props and/or images, if required (see also the **Performance Ideas and Storytelling Suggestions** above).

After the reading, check that the children understand any new or difficult words (see **Key Vocabulary** above).

Ask questions to check the children's understanding of the poem. These can be open to group discussion or children can pair with talk partners before reporting back to the group. For example:

- *How does the apple taste and look?*
- *Where are the pips?*

- *How do the pips look and feel?*
- *Where is the pip/seed planted?*
- *What helps the pip/seed to grow into a tree?*
- *From where will the plants get their light?* (From the sun; show an image of the sun as a prompt, if necessary.)
- *How does the person in the poem get an apple?*
- *Why do you think the person wants to eat an apple from their apple tree?*

Say the poem one more time. Slow down and allow the children to predict and say end-rhyming or main words with you (for example, 'hand', 'bite', 'white', 'core', 'pips', 'brown', 'ground', 'grows and grows', 'rain', 'light' and/or 'apple tree').

Extra consolidation activity

Drawing and describing an apple

- Give pairs of children an apple and some paper.
- Let them look at the apple and then individually draw and colour in what they see.
- Ask them to describe their drawings to their partners.
- Add the apples to a pre-prepared paper or card apple tree with several branches (attached to a display board).

EXPLORING THE POEM

PHASE 2: Getting to know the poem

Session 3: Let's get to know the poem 👥👥 👥👥

Show the children an apple and a pip, and remind them of the poem. Ask them what they remember about it. Retell the poem using the **Storyteller** video on **Connect**, or by displaying the poem and reading it aloud using hand actions. Then retell the poem again, asking the children to join in with words and/or actions.

After the second retelling, choose focus activities to explore the poem in more depth.

'Structure focus' activities

Sequencing different parts of the poem 👥👥 👥👥

- Display the interactive activity 'The Apple'.
- Click on the first audio speaker to hear the first part of the poem. Ask the children which image should be dragged into the first box.
- Repeat this process with each audio speaker and box, until all the images are in place.
- Discuss each section, noting how the beginnings and ends are the same.
- Listen again to the poem and discuss with the children which part(s) they like most and why.

Sequencing how apples grow 👥👥 👥👥

- Retell the part of the poem that focuses on how apples are grown. Act it out, or use hand actions, to help illustrate the sequence.
- To consolidate understanding of this process, display the images on Resource Sheet 7.1 in a mixed-up order, and encourage the children to sort the images into the correct sequence.

Differentiation: Encourage more confident children to discuss and create a further sequence of how apples could get to the shops (for example, on lorries).

'Vocabulary focus' activities

Describing apples 👥👥 👥👥

- Point out the words used to describe the first apple in the poem.
- Ask the children to suggest words to describe how the next apple could taste, feel and look. Orally model a few words such as 'mushy', 'crisp', 'soft', 'pinkish' and 'yellow', and then write them down.
- Let the children discuss their words with mixed-ability talk partners before feeding back their ideas to the group. Record their suggestions onto apple shapes cut from craft paper for their tree display (or use them for the 'class apple poem' activity, below).

Composing a class apple poem 👥👥 👥👥

- Draw a large apple shape on craft paper, to create a large apple shape-poem.
- Say the first lines of the poem, and write them above the shape: 'I hold an apple in my hand, and take a bite. Inside it is… '
- With the children's prompting, write their descriptive words from the 'describing apples' activity, above. Read the final poem back to the children and encourage them to join in.

Differentiation: More confident children may wish to try to sound out and write their own words in the shape.

'Phonics focus' activity

CVC: Investigating 'p-i-p' 👥👥 👥👥

- Show a pip to the children. Ask them what it is. Write out the word and point to each letter as you sound out each phoneme before saying the word.
- Display the interactive activity 'What Is Inside the Pip?'
- Look at the different pips on the screen and click on each one to reveal an '–ip' word.
- Encourage the children to join in with the sounding and blending of CVC words ending in 'i-p' (for example, 'tip', 'lip', 'sip', 'hip', 'dip', 'zip').

For more work on CVC and CCVC words that end with 'i-p', see the 'Phonics Work' section under 'Literacy Activities', below.

EXPLORING THE POEM

PHASE 3: Performing the poem

Session 4: Let's put on a performance 👥 👥

Remind the children of their work so far. Show the poem again using the **Storyteller** video on **Connect**, or retell it with the children from the whiteboard, using the hand gestures or miming the actions. Then create a performance of the poem by splitting the class into three groups, each allocated a different part of the poem:

- Ask the first group to look at acting out the poem up to finding the pips.
- Ask the second group to look at acting out the poem up to planting the pips with the rain and light.
- Ask the third group to look at acting out the poem up to the growth of an apple tree.
- Ask all three groups then to look at acting out the section of the poem about picking an apple and eating it.
- Encourage each group to recite lines, or end words or phrases, as well as using actions and/or hand signals. If possible, film their performance for the children to watch and enjoy.

LITERACY ACTIVITIES

Reading

Matching tree labels

- Ask mixed-ability pairs to work on the interactive activity 'Parts of an Apple Tree', matching and dragging the correct labels to the different parts of the apple tree.

Differentiation: Suggest that less confident readers focus on the initial highlighted letter sounds of each label. More confident readers should take a lead in blending sounds, encouraging less confident readers to join in.

Exploring and labelling apples

- Ask small groups, with adult supervision, to explore and investigate the different parts of an apple: stem, pips, peel or skin, core and flesh or fruit.
- Once each group has discussed the different parts, the supervising adult should write labels for the children to sound out, read and match to the correct apple sections.

Differentiation: Ask early or less confident readers to use their fingers to count out each phoneme of the apple parts as they are supported in blending sounds. Support them as they sound out the letters on the labels.

Finding apple information

- Provide a selection of picture and information books about apples and apple trees for the children to explore and, if appropriate, read with an adult.

Finding the missing words

- Ask groups or pairs to use the interactive activity 'Apple Sentences', selecting the correct missing words to complete the sentences about apples.

Writing

Finding uses for apples

- Ask mixed-ability pairs to use the interactive activity 'What Can We Do with Apples?', selecting the missing words to complete the sentences.

Making pip letters

- If enough apple pips are available, ask the children to use pips to form and spell out words connected to the poem (for example, 'pip', 'hand', 'root', 'apple' or 'rain').
- The pips could be stuck down once a letter or word is formed, or put away for other activities.

Creating apple cards

- Explain how apples can be used to say 'thank you' (traditionally, to teachers!).
- Ask the children to design their own thank-you cards for anyone of their choice, using cut-out pictures of apples. With support as needed, ask each child to write a short message and their name in their card.

Differentiation: Scribe less confident children's messages, but encourage them to write their names and prompt them to sound out and segment selected words.

Giving apples names

- Discuss the names of different kinds of apples. Write 'pippin' and 'russet', and model sounding and blending the letters and phonemes.
- Show an apple, and give it a simple, new CVC name. Model blending the letters as you write it out.
- Ask groups or pairs to think up their own CVC apple names, and to share them with the class.
- Work together to sound out and write each name on the whiteboard.

Differentiation: More confident writers could write out their own apple names independently.

Making labels

- Ask the children to complete the interactive activity 'Fruit and Vegetable Stall', dragging the correct letters to complete the labels for the fruit and vegetables.

Phonics Work

CVC phonemes

- Cut a set of pip-shaped cards from craft paper, and have them to hand.
- Use the top one to write 'pip' and sound out each phoneme with the children: 'p-i-p'.
- Ask the children to think of other words that end with 'i-p' (for example, 'rip', 'tip' or 'sip').
- Ask them to sound out the words (and write them on the cards, with support as necessary).

Differentiation: More confident children could look at CCVC words (such as 'trip' and 'slip').

/ee/ and /oo/

- Encourage more confident children to explore the phonic letter/sound correspondences for /ee/ (as in 'sweet') and the long vowel sound /oo/ (as in 'root').
- Highlight that the apple in the poem was 'sweet'. Say the word 'sweet' again, and then sound it out as you write it.
- Underline the graphemes 'ee' and say the sound /ee/ with the children. Let them sound out 'deep' as you write it out.
- Do the same with the letter/sound correspondence for the long vowel sound /oo/, focusing on the words 'root' and 'smooth'.
- In small groups or pairs, ask the children to make lists of all the words they can that contain these spellings. Then ask them to share their lists.

CROSS-CURRICULAR ACTIVITIES

Adult-led activities 👥

Cooking (PSHE)

- With adult supervision, the children follow a simple recipe using apples, such as for an apple tart or a fruit salad.

Differentiation: Encourage more confident children to look at the layout of the recipe and recount the sequence of what to do.

Investigating apples (Understanding the World)

- Ask groups to conduct an apple investigation, using their senses to sort different apples into groups (for example, using smell, colour, taste, texture – outer and inner – and sound of the first bite).
- The investigation could be recorded using pictures or a scribe.

Differentiation: More confident children could try and write some of their own words to record the investigation.

Planting apple pips/seeds (Understanding the World)

Have an apple-pip growing session:

- Highlight that pips initially need cold to help them grow.
- Place some pips on a damp paper towel and seal them in a container or plastic bag.
- Leave them to germinate in the fridge for up to eight weeks, and then plant them in a pot.

Apple tasting graphs (Mathematics)

- Have a group tasting session, tasting red, green and golden apples. Encourage groups to discuss which apple they liked most and why.
- Draw a block graph and ask children for their responses to complete it. Which coloured apple was the favourite?

Child-led activities 👥 👥

Apple art (Expressive Arts)

- Have an apple-printing session, using paints and paper.
- The children could make a collage picture by gluing their apple prints to a pre-prepared image of an apple tree.

Shopping for apples (Communication and Language; Understanding the World)

- Children role-play shopping for apples in a shop or at a stall. Encourage them to think about why they want these apples and how many they would need for what they have in mind.

Transporting apples (Communication and Language; Understanding the World)

- Ask children to use small-world toys to role-play apples being picked and packed, transported by lorry or ship to the shops, and sold.

Apple counting (Mathematics)

- Use apples or apple pips/seeds for counting games such as 'How many pips/seeds in an apple?'.
- Children could also sort or order apples by size or shape.

SEQUENCE ASSESSMENT

Communication and Language

- Does the child listen and respond to discussion about the poem?
- Does the child listen and join in with the retelling of the poem?
- Does the child use talk to organise, sequence and clarify thinking and ideas about the poem and the related poem activities?
- Does the child show evidence of extending their vocabulary?

Reading

- Can the child hear initial sounds for words relating to different parts of an apple?
- Can the child segment and blend sounds in words relating to apples?
- Can the child segment and blend sounds for words ending in 'i-p'?
- Can the child sound out and blend the long vowel phonemes /ee/ and /oo/?

Writing

- Can the child write labels for parts of the apple (for example, skin, pip, core)?
- Can the child segment sounds for words relating to apples and write them down?
- Can the child write a simple caption for an apple card?
- Can the child write simple sentences using words ending 'i-p' and including the long vowel phonemes /ee/ and /oo/?

Review of the Big Picture

At the end of this sequence, discuss with the children what they liked about the poem 'The Apple'. Ask: *Which section or words or phrases did you like? What do you now know about apples, apple pips and how apples grow? Discuss what new words you have learnt about apples.*

Encourage each child to show and explain examples of their writing and reading achievements, and any cross-curricular activities they enjoyed.

Use the 'Pupil observation chart' to record each child's responses and attainment.

SEQUENCE 8 Food: Growing Food

TERM 2 (SPRING): 1st half term

Main Topic:	Food
Subtopic:	Growing Food
Text Type:	Story
Main Source Text:	*The Enormous Potato* by Aubrey Davis (ISBN 978-1-550-74669-3)
Extra Source Texts:	*The Gigantic Turnip* by Aleksei Tolstoy (ISBN 978-1-905-23672-5); *The Big Turnip* by Monica Hughes (ISBN 978-0-007-18644-0)
Approximate Duration:	Two weeks

Big Picture

During this sequence, children will listen to the story 'The Enormous Potato' and discuss its events, structure and vocabulary as a group. They will also have the opportunity to explore the characters and events through role-play.

Through a range of supportive activities, the children will have the opportunity to explore more about the story's characters and about growing and using potatoes.

Phonics Focuses

The children will use their knowledge of letter sounds to blend and segment VC and CVCC/CCVC words. They will also explore words containing the graphemes 'ii', 'ch' and 'ow', and use their sounds to blend words.

Learning Outcomes: See 'Learning Outcomes' Chart, on pages xi–xiv.

Key Vocabulary: enormous, potato, farmer, potato eye, ground, town

Home Links

Encourage children to:

- notice how often, and in what varieties, they eat potatoes
- look at the different potatoes on display in shops
- plant and grow potatoes.

Resources Required

Workbook Pages: 4–14, 17–20, 29–30

Resource Sheets 8.1–8.2: 'The Enormous Potato' Storyboard; Who Pulled the Potato?

General Resources:

- A selection of potatoes, one of which is sprouting
- Sticky tack
- Craft paper
- One larger and three smaller boxes
- Potato-print letters (carved in advance)
- Paint
- Mixing bowls and spoons
- Potato salad ingredients: boiled new potatoes, mayonnaise, chopped spring onions, chives, capers and/or cornichons, salt and pepper
- Craft materials (e.g. balloons, glue, newspapers, paint, pens, pipe cleaners)

Background Knowledge

Explain to the children that:

- 'The Enormous Potato' is a version of a traditional tale called 'The Big Turnip'
- a potato, like a turnip, grows under the soil
- a potato plant is generally ready to be dug up when its green, leafy shoots appear above the soil. There are many different types of potato, which can be used and cooked in many different ways
- the 'eye' of a potato is one of the little spots on a potato that can sprout into roots (the children may have seen old potatoes beginning to sprout roots)
- potato plants grow from the 'eye' of another potato.

Performance Ideas and Storytelling Suggestions

★ Read through the story out loud to yourself before reading it to the class, to help you decide where you could add emphasis and intonation to key words or lines (for example, using different voices or inflections for the different characters).

★ Use actions and facial expressions to bring the story to life (for example, huffing and puffing with the pulling of the potato plant).

★ If possible, show an enlarged image of a very large potato when it is pulled out so that the children can compare it with a normal potato.

Sequence Structure

This chart offers suggestions on the order and timings of exploring the story over a two-week period. However, please feel free to adapt the sessions to your own planning and suitable timings for your whole class or set groups.

Exploring the Story

Tip: If possible, aim to read or show the story to the children regularly over the two-week period, or before any related activity, so that the children get to know the story and its messages well.

WEEK 1 (PHASE 1)	WEEKS 1–2 (PHASE 2)	WEEKS 1–2 (PHASE 3)
Introduction to the story	**Getting to know the story**	**Performing the story**
All sections could be done in one session or split over two or three sessions.	Aim to hold one or two sessions on getting to know the story, each retelling the story and then including your own choice of activities.	Aim to hold one or two sessions at different times across the two-week period.
1. **What do we know?** (15–20 minutes) 2. **Let's listen and talk** (approx. 30 minutes) **Extra consolidation activity:** • The potato party (approx. 20 minutes)	3. **Let's get to know the story** (10–15 minutes) **'Structure focus' activity:** • 'The Enormous Potato' storyboard (approx. 15 minutes) • Growing and using potatoes (approx. 15 minutes) **'Vocabulary focus' activity:** • 'Big' words (15–20 minutes) **'Phonics focus' activity:** • Pulling out the 'll' words (approx. 10 minutes)	4. **Let's put on a performance** (20–30 minutes)

Literacy Activities

READING	WRITING	PHONICS WORK
• 'What an Enormous Potato!' • Who pulled the potato?	• Potato-print writing • Word rope • My favourite potato dish	• Hot potato • 'ch' and 'ow'

Cross-curricular Activities

Adult-led activities:	Child-led activities:
• Growing potatoes (Understanding the World) • Songs and stories (Expressive Arts; Mathematics) • Making potato salad (PSHE, Physical Development) • Looking at potatoes (Understanding the World, Communication and Language)	• Balloon potatoes (Expressive Arts) • Potato characters (Expressive Arts; Communication and Language) • Sorting potatoes (Mathematics) • Small-world shopping (Communication and Language)

Sequence Assessment

• Communication and Language
• Reading
• Writing
• Review of the Big Picture

EXPLORING THE STORY

PHASE 1: Introduction to the story

Session 1: What do we know?

Show the children a potato with a small shoot coming from it. Ask questions to find out what they know about potatoes. For example:

- *What is this?*
- *How do we often use it?* (Encourage knowledge of foods such as chips and baked potatoes.)
- *Where can we get potatoes?* (shops, gardens, allotments, and so on)
- *How do you think potatoes grow?*

Discuss the **Background Knowledge** given above, and show the children the eye on the potato. Ensure children understand that potatoes' eyes do not see. Ask why the children think these may be called 'eyes'.

Then explain to the children that they are going to listen to a story about a farmer who grows a potato and spend time doing lots of fun activities that will explore the story and potatoes.

Session 2: Let's listen and talk

Remind the children briefly of their discussion about potatoes. Introduce the story 'The Enormous Potato' by asking the children what they think 'enormous' means. Say the word with added emphasis, to give them a clue. Let them join in, saying 'The **Enormous** Potato', and use arm movements to indicate the size.

Show the video for 'The Enormous Potato' on **Connect**, or read the story yourself (see the **Performance Ideas and Storytelling Suggestions** above).

After the reading, check that the children understand any new or difficult words (see **Key Vocabulary** above).

Ask questions to check the children's understanding of the story. These can be open to group discussion or children can pair with talk partners before reporting back to the group. For example:

- *What did the farmer plant?*
- *How did the potato grow?*
- *How did the farmer try to get the potato out?*

- *Who did the farmer's wife call to help them?*
- *Which animals helped the farmer to pull up the potato?*
- *What did they do to the potato?*
- *What did the people from town bring with them?*
- *What was left of the potato at the end?*

Finally, ask the children whether or not they believe that the farmer was glad he tried to grow the potato and to explain why they think this. Link the discussion back to where the children would usually find potatoes, and how they get from farms to shops and restaurants.

Extra consolidation activity

The potato party

- Display 'The Enormous Potato Party' from **Connect**.
- Point out and ask questions about how the potato was being prepared for cooking (being cut, peeled, chopped) and the different ways it was being cooked (boiling, frying, baking).
- Point to different people in the picture, and ask talk partners to decide what they could be saying. Give examples to begin the discussion (for example, 'Yummy!'/'Delicious!'/'I want more!'/'This is the best chip ever!').

EXPLORING THE STORY

PHASE 2: Getting to know the story

Session 3: Let's get to know the story 👥👥 👥👥

Show the children the shooting potato again, and remind them of the story. Ask them what they remember about it. Retell the story using the **Storyteller** video on **Connect**, or by reading it aloud to the class.

Encourage the children to join in with the repetitive phrasing for the grabbing and pulling of the potato, the sounds of the animals and the 'rip' of the potato coming out.

After the retelling, choose focus activities to explore the story in more depth.

'Structure focus' activities

'The Enormous Potato' storyboard 👥👥 👥👥

- Print and cut out the images from Resource Sheet 8.1 and put sticky tack on their backs. Have craft paper available as a display area for the images.
- Place the images in a mixed-up order.
- Encourage the children to create a storyboard of 'The Enormous Potato' by putting the images into the correct order.
- Once the storyboard is complete, ask groups to retell the story.
- Display the storyboard in the room for reference.

Growing and using potatoes 👥👥 👥👥

- Display the interactive activity 'Growing and Using Potatoes'.
- Look at each image with the children and discuss what is happening.
- Ask the children to help you drag the images into the correct order, ensuring you and they use the right vocabulary (for example, 'eye', 'dig', 'shoots').
- Afterwards, ask talk partners to discuss the sequence.

'Vocabulary focus' activity

'Big' words 👥👥 👥👥

- Remind the children how big the potato grew to be.
- Ask them if they can remind you what word is used to describe this ('enormous').
- Ask what other words could be used to mean 'very big', giving prompts as necessary (for example, 'huge', 'gigantic', 'massive', 'large').
- Say each of the words with the children, with emphasis to make the words sound big.
- Ask talk partners to decide which 'big' word they would choose to describe the potato.

Differentiation: Fast finishers could also look at 'small' words, connecting them to a small potato or to the little mouse in the story.

'Phonics focus' activity

Pulling out the 'll' words 👥👥 👥👥

- Create word cards for decodable words that end in –ell, –ill and –oll (for example, 'well', 'bell', 'will', 'mill' and 'doll'), and put them in a box. Set out three smaller boxes labelled '–ell', '–ill' and '–oll'.
- Write out the word 'pull' and point to the 'll'. Explain that, although the letter L appears twice, the sound is the same as made by one L. Sound out 'pull' and ask the children to copy you.
- Ask children to take turns to pull a word card from the box. Ask the class to chant 'pull' as they do it, and encourage the child to pretend they are pulling hard.
- Hold up the card and ask the children to segment and blend the letters and sounds, with emphasis on the 'll' grapheme.
- Ask the children in which pot the word belongs and let them put the card into the correct pot.

Differentiation: More confident children could use longer 'll' words, such as 'smell', 'still' and 'troll'.

EXPLORING THE STORY

PHASE 3: Performing the story

Session 4: Let's put on a performance 👥 👥

Over the two weeks, encourage the children to explore the story through role-play. For example:

- Ask the children to play the roles of the farmer and his family, trying to get the enormous potato out of the ground. Let them pretend to grab the green shoots and pull. How else could they get the potato out? Suggest ideas (such as pushing, using a rope, digging).
- Ask the children to play the people from the town, and to act out hearing about the enormous potato, before discussing how they will cook and eat it.

During the final session, remind the children of their work so far. Show the story again using the **Storyteller** video on **Connect**, or retell it with the children from the whiteboard. Then ask the children to work together to act out the story.

- Allocate the roles of characters from the story to some children. You may want to add more to the line of people pulling (for example, a son, grandparent, goat or cow). You may even wish to allocate the role of the potato!
- Ask the other children to become people from the town, and to improvise hearing about, hurrying to, cooking and eating the potato.
- Read out the story as the children perform their roles. Encourage them to join in with any repetitive phrasing or speech.

LITERACY ACTIVITIES

Reading

What an Enormous Potato!

- Ask mixed-ability pairs to work on the interactive activity 'What an Enormous Potato!', completing the sentences with the missing word after an audio prompt.

Differentiation: More confident readers attempt to read the action words without listening to the audio prompts.

Who pulled the potato?

- Cut out the tiles from Resource Sheet 8.2. Display the large potato at the end of a long line or paper strip, and lay out the other images face down.
- Ask each child to select one image, and to segment and blend the sounds on the label to form the word featured.
- Then ask the child to add it to the potato line, saying 'The… grabbed the potato!'
- When all the images have been added, assist the children to read out the labels and end the sentence with '… grabbed the potato!'

Differentiation: Make slightly more advanced word character cards for more confident readers.

Writing

Potato-print writing

- Supply potato-print letters, paint and craft paper.
- Ask the children to use the potato-print letters to create words, first selecting the letters they need to create given words related to the story such as 'pull', 'grab', 'dog' and 'cook'.

Differentiation: Give less confident writers the correct potato letters for a word. Encourage them to sound and blend them into the word.

Word rope

- Ask mixed-ability pairs to work on the interactive activity 'Word Rope', dragging the letters to complete the words on the rope after an audio prompt.

Differentiation: Suggest that more confident readers create oral sentences using the –ot words and then write them down.

My favourite potato dish

- Discuss the children's favourite potato dishes.
- Ask them to draw or find images of their selection.
- Write out the words 'I like', and ask the children to read aloud and have a go at writing these words themselves.
- Help each child to sound out and spell the name of their favourite potato dish before they write it down to complete their sentence.

Differentiation: More confident writers could try to blend and write their words independently.

Phonics Work

Hot potato

- Ask groups to sit in circles.
- Give each group a potato. Ask them to pretend that the potato is hot.
- Say a CVC word such as 'cat' and ask the children to think of other words that end in '–at'.
- Give examples to help them before the game starts (for example, 'mat', 'pat', 'rat').
- When a child is passed the potato, they should say their word.
- Stop the potato to suggest another VC spelling group (for example, '–op') when appropriate.

'ch' and 'ow'

- Ask mixed-ability pairs to work on the interactive activity 'Words with 'ow' and 'ch'', matching the images to the words containing 'ch' or 'ow'.

Differentiation: Encourage more confident children to think of other words that contain these sounds.

CROSS-CURRICULAR ACTIVITIES

Adult-led activities 👥

Growing potatoes (Understanding the World)

Work with the children to start growing potatoes:

- Collect or store potatoes until sprouts appear from the eyes.
- Bury the potatoes in the ground (or in a deep container).
- Make sure they have lots of sun and some water.
- If you plant them in spring, you should have potatoes by early summer.

Songs and stories (Expressive Arts; Mathematics)

- Teach the children rhymes relating to vegetables, such as the old counting rhyme 'One Potato, Two Potato'. This rhyme can also be used as a fun way to select a child to do something.
- Read and share the original traditional tale 'The Big Turnip'. Using the similarities between the stories, ask children to think up their own version (for example, 'The Huge Carrot').

Making potato salad (PSHE, Physical Development)

- To make a simple potato salad, ask the children to mix the cooked potatoes with mayonnaise, and then to flavour their salad using seasoning and spring onions, chives, capers and/or cornichons.
- Suggest that the children try each other's salads and discuss the tastes.

Looking at potatoes (Understanding the World, Communication and Language)

- Bring in a selection of potatoes for the children to examine in more detail.
- Suggest various ways the children can explore and compare the differences between the potatoes (for example, their sizes, shapes, textures, colours, names and, if cooked, tastes).

Child-led activities 👥 👥

Balloon potatoes (Expressive Arts)

- Blow up a balloon for each child, and ask the children to add strips of paper soaked in glue paste to cover their balloons. For best effect, suggest they add two or three layers.
- Place the balloons somewhere safe to dry, and then pop the balloons.
- Encourage the children to paint their balloon shapes in white and brown to look like big potatoes.

Potato characters (Expressive Arts; Communication and Language)

- Give the children potatoes to make into characters from the story, using craft materials. They could choose to use the potato as just the head or as the whole body of their chosen character.
- Eyes, ears and nose stickers can be stuck on using glue.
- Use pipe cleaners or card to make legs, arms and tails.
- The children can also use a range of materials to decorate the potato characters such as sequins, glitter, paint, feathers, wool and cloth.

Sorting potatoes (Mathematics)

- Bring in a selection of potatoes for the children to examine in more detail.
- Leave the children to conduct different maths investigations, such as sorting the potatoes into size, from small to large, or predicting which will be the heaviest potato and then weighing them.

Small-world shopping (Communication and Language)

- Encourage the children to act out scenarios based around a potato stall using small-world figures.
- They could also use small-world equipment to retell the story.

SEQUENCE ASSESSMENT

Communication and Language
- Does the child listen to the story with increasing attention and recall?
- Does the child anticipate key events in the story?
- Does the child use talk to organise, sequence and clarify thinking and ideas about the story?
- Does the child show evidence of extending their vocabulary?
- Does the child introduce and explore the story in their play?

Reading
- Can the child join in with the repeated refrains in 'The Enormous Potato'?
- Can the child anticipate key events and phrases in the story?
- Can the child hear and say the initial sounds in CVC, CVCC and CCVC words?
- Can the child segment the sounds in simple words and blend them together?
- Can the child segment the sounds for 'll' and 'ch' and blend them in words?

Writing
- Can the child segment and blend sounds for words relating to the story and write them down?
- Can the child recognise and write down initial letters in CVC/CVCC/CCVC words?
- Can the child write short sentences?

Review of the Big Picture
At the end of this sequence, discuss with the children what they liked about the story 'The Enormous Potato'. Encourage them to retell the story using the storyboard. Ask: *What part did you like most? What have you learnt about potatoes and how they are grown? What new words and sounds have you learnt over the two weeks?*

Encourage each child to show and explain examples of their writing and reading achievements, and any cross-curricular activities they enjoyed.

Use the 'Pupil observation chart' to record each child's responses and attainment.

SEQUENCE 9 Food: Growing Plants

TERM 2 (SPRING): 1st half term

Main Topic:	Food
Subtopic:	Growing Plants
Text Type:	rhyme/poem
Main Source Text:	*Juba's Bean* by Alison Milford
Extra Source Text:	*Jack and the Beanstalk* by Iona Treahy (ISBN 978-1-409-30959-8)
Approximate Duration:	Two weeks

Big Picture

During this sequence, children will listen to and join in with the rhyme 'Juba's Beanstalk' which is set to the well-known nursery rhyme, 'Here we go round the mulberry bush'. They have the opportunity to discuss the rhyme's message, look at its repetitive structure and explore the characters and events more through role-play. They will also work on learning the names of the days of the week and their order.

Through a range of supportive activities, the children will have the opportunity to explore more about growing and using beans.

Phonics Focuses

The children will investigate CVC words and different VC spelling patterns, and use initial letters to help them to read and write simple words. They will also explore words containing the grapheme 'ai' and use its sound to blend words.

Learning Outcomes: See 'Learning Outcomes' Chart, on pages xi–xiv.

Key Vocabulary: days of the week, water, soil, slug, snail, billy goat, scarecrow, stew, beanstalk

Home Links

Encourage children to:
- listen to the story of 'Jack and the Beanstalk'
- find out more about West Africa (Nigeria) and family subsistence farming on vegetable plots
- look at different beans and ways they are used at home
- plant and grow beans.

Resources Required

Workbook Pages: 4–12, 21–22, 29–30

Resource Sheets 9.1–9.2: Beanstalk Sentences; The Snail Game

General Resources:
- A large bean (such as a broad bean)
- Image of a beanstalk
- Images of family vegetable plots and subsistence farming in Nigeria
- Map of world to show where Nigeria is (optional)
- Craft paper
- Counters and a 1–4 spinner
- Bean bags
- Glass jars containing damp cotton wool
- Craft materials (e.g. newspaper, tape, glue, paint, pens, pipe cleaners, cloth)
- A selection of different beans (e.g. broad, runner, haricot), including lots of dried beans
- Clean plastic drinks bottles
- Green tights

Background Knowledge

Explain to the children that:
- the rhyme tune of 'Juba's Bean' is the same as 'Here we go round the mulberry bush'. Sing the nursery rhyme for or with the children so that they can hear the rhythm and repetitive structure
- the rhyme is set in West Africa in a country called Nigeria. If possible, show where Nigeria is on a world map compared to the UK. Show images of a Nigerian rural area where crops and vegetables are grown
- beanstalks grow from beans and also produce beans, which grow on their leafy stalks
- like many plants, bean plants take a long time to grow and require patience.

Performance Ideas and Storytelling Suggestions

- ★ Read through the rhyme out loud to yourself before reading it to the class, to help you decide where you could add emphasis and intonation to key words or lines.

- ★ Add emphasis to days of the week and the repetitive second and third lines. Say the last lines of each verse slowly so that the children can hear the reasons behind the actions.

- ★ Use the poem sheet to help you with the body actions or use your own ideas. Make them clear for children to copy and use.

Sequence Structure

This chart offers suggestions on the order and timings of exploring the rhyme over a two-week period. However, please feel free to adapt the sessions to your own planning and suitable timings for your whole class or set groups.

Exploring the Rhyme

Tip: If possible, aim to read or show the rhyme to the children regularly over the two-week period, or before any related activity, so that the children get to know the rhyme and its messages well.

WEEK 1 (PHASE 1)	WEEKS 1–2 (PHASE 2)	WEEKS 1–2 (PHASE 3)
Introduction to the rhyme	**Getting to know the rhyme**	**Performing the rhyme**
The first session would work well conducted separately from the second session and extra consolidation activity.	Aim to hold one or two sessions on getting to know the rhyme, each reciting the rhyme and then including your own choice of activities.	These sessions could be rehearsed and performed at different times across the week.
1. **What do we know?** (20–30 minutes) 2. **Let's listen and talk** (approx. 30 minutes) **Extra consolidation activity:** • Waiting for things to happen (20–30 minutes)	3. **Let's get to know the rhyme** (15–20 minutes) **'Structure focus' activity:** • Juba's bean (approx. 15 minutes) **'Vocabulary focus' activity:** • Juba's 'days of the week' song (approx. 15 minutes) **'Phonics focus' activity:** • A bug on the beanstalk (approx. 10 minutes)	4. • **Let's put on a performance** • **Exploring the rhyme through mime and movement** (20-25 minutes) • **Class performance** (20-25 minutes) • **Growing and climbing** (15–20 minutes)

Literacy Activities

READING	WRITING	PHONICS WORK
• Juba's vegetable plot • Creature cards • Beanstalk sentences	• The top of the beanstalk • Bean words	• The snail game • Juba's scarecrow

Cross-curricular Activities

Adult-led activities:	Child-led activities:
• Growing beanstalks (Understanding the World) • Bean games (Physical Development) • Beanstalk displays (Expressive Arts) • Beans for meals (Understanding the World; PSHE)	• Bean shakers (Expressive Arts) • Beanstalk corner (Communication and Language) • Bean hunting (PSHE; Mathematics)

Sequence Assessment

• Communication and Language
• Reading
• Writing
• Review of the Big Picture

EXPLORING THE RHYME

PHASE 1: Introduction to the rhyme

Session 1: What do we know? 👥 👥

Show the children a large bean. Ask questions and give prompts to assess their current knowledge about beans and how they grow. For example:

- *What do you think this is?*
- *How do we often use it?* (Encourage knowledge of foods such as baked or runner beans.)
- *Where can we get beans?* (shops, gardens, allotments, and so on)
- *What do you think it will grow into?* (a beanstalk) Show the children an image of a grown beanstalk.

Discuss the **Background Knowledge** given above, and ask questions to ascertain children's knowledge of the traditional tale 'Jack and the Beanstalk'. Retell a simple version of the story, emphasising the fact that Jack's beans were magic, and grew very quickly. Ask children how long they think real beans take to grow into beanstalks. (They take around two weeks.)

Then explain to the children that they are going to listen to a rhyme about growing a real (not magical!) beanstalk from a bean, spend time doing lots of fun activities that will explore the rhyme and beans.

Session 2: Let's listen and talk 👥 👥 👥

Show the children the bean again, and remind them briefly of their discussion about beans and Jack and the Beanstalk. Explain that they are going to listen to a rhyme about a girl called Juba from Nigeria in West Africa who wants to grow a big beanstalk from one bean. Highlight that the rhyme is the same as the nursery rhyme, 'Here we go round the mulberry bush'. Sing a verse of the rhyme for the children to hear the rhythm and repetitive pattern.

Show the **Storyteller** video for 'Juba's Bean' on **Connect**, or read the rhyme yourself (see the **Performance Ideas and Storytelling Suggestions** above).

After the reading, check that the children understand any new or difficult words (see **Key Vocabulary** above).

Ask questions to check the children's understanding of the rhyme with reference to the verses and the illustrations. These can be open to group discussion or children can pair with talk partners before reporting back to the group. For example:

- *Who gave Juba a bean on Monday?*
- *What did she use to water the soil?*

- *Why did she move the slugs and snails from the bean?*
- *Why did the goats need to be scared off?*
- *What popped up when the sun came out?*
- *Why was Juba sad on Sunday?*
- *How long did Gran say the the beanstalk will take to grow?* (Encourage the children to say, 'a little while longer'.)
- *What did Juba cook Gran with the beans from the beanstalk?*
- *How do we know Juba doesn't live in the UK?* (Focus on the illustrations.)

Say the rhyme one more time. Let the children join in with the actions and the repetitive lines. If possible, let the children say the repetitive second and third lines without adult participation. You could say the rhyme one more time to see if they can remember and say the last non-repetitive line.

Extra consolidation activity

Waiting for things to happen 👥 👥 👥

- Remind the children that Juba felt sad and fed up because her bean did not grow in a week.
- Discuss the length of one week with the children, linking it to their school routine (and using a calendar to show their week for visual help, if needed).
- Discuss how difficult it is to wait for things to happen when you are excited about them. Share a personal experience of this.
- Encourage talk partners to share their own experiences of having to wait for an exciting event, before asking them to feed back to the group.

EXPLORING THE RHYME

PHASE 2: Getting to know the rhyme

Session 3: Let's get to know the rhyme 👥 👥

Show the children the bean again, and remind them of the rhyme. Ask them what they remember about it. Retell the rhyme using the **Storyteller** video on **Connect**, or read out the rhyme again yourself. After the retelling, choose focus activities to explore the rhyme in more depth.

'Structure focus' activity

Juba's bean 👥 👥

- Display the interactive activity 'Juba's bean'.
- Remind the children how Juba hoped that her bean would grow quickly.
- Ask the children to help you put the pictures into the right order by retelling or singing the rhyme. Say each day out loud to reinforce day order.
- Drag the pictures into the correct order as the rhyme is being retold or sung.
- Once the activity has been completed, go through what happened in the rhyme and how it ended.

'Vocabulary focus' activity

Juba's 'days of the week' song 👥 👥

- Sing the song below to the tune of 'Twinkle, Twinkle, Little Star'.

  On Monday, Tuesday, Wednesday, Thursday,
  Friday, Saturday and on Sunday,
  Juba really wants to know
  Why her bean won't grow and grow.
  Monday, Tuesday, Wednesday, Thursday
  Friday, Saturday and then Sunday.

- Use the song to help the children to learn and remember the names and order of the days of the week.
- Provide word cards for the days, with the initial letters highlighted and sing again. Ask children holding the cards to stand in the right order and to hold up the cards as the days are mentioned.

'Phonics focus' activity

A bug on the beanstalk 👥 👥

- Display the interactive activity 'Beanstalk Word Tree'.
- Point to the VC pattern '–ug' at the top of the beanstalk, and sound and blend it out.
- Explain that you will be adding letters in front of these ones to make words.
- Point to the example image and the word 'bug'. Sound it out with the children.
- Point to the other '–ug' leaves and ask the children to think of other words that end in '–ug' (for example, 'tug', 'mug', 'dug').
- Type in the letters to create the words.

Differentiation: For more confident children, create other beanstalk word family trees for display boards. The children can then write out and add word cards for each family.

EXPLORING THE RHYME

PHASE 3: Performing the rhyme

Session 4: Let's put on a performance

Over the two weeks, encourage the children to explore the rhyme, through role-play.

During the final session, remind the children of their work so far. Show the rhyme again using the **Storyteller** video on **Connect**, or retell it with the children from the whiteboard. Then ask the children to work together to explore an element of the rhyme in more depth. Focuses for different groups could include:

Exploring the rhyme through mime and movement

- Sing or tell each verse of the rhyme and encourage the children to be Juba, miming her actions for each verse.
- Allow children to take their time acting out Juba's physical actions in each verse, such as planting the bean, watering the bean and soil, moving slugs and snails, making a scarecrow, picking beans and cooking bean stew in a pot.
- Encourage them to use their faces and bodies to convey Juba's changing emotions, such as happiness, annoyance over the slugs, pride over the scarecrow, sadness over the beanstalk, happiness at giving Gran the stew.

Class performance

- Encourage the children to join in with the rhyme, focusing on the repetitive phrases for the first four lines.
- Encourage them to use the physical and facial actions as cues to help them remember the words.
- Put the children into nine groups and give them each a verse to say and perform. Different children in each group could say a line or the group could say the lines together.
- Have a class performance with either a simple retelling of the rhyme or using actions as each verse is said.

Growing and climbing

- Ask the children to pretend to be beans, gradually growing and stretching until they are tall beanstalks.
- Suggest that they have grown huge, magic beanstalks, like the one in 'Jack and the Beanstalk', and ask them to mime climbing upwards.

LITERACY ACTIVITIES

Reading

Juba's vegetable plot

- Ask mixed-ability pairs to work on the interactive activity 'Juba's Vegetable Plot', adding the missing word to each sentence after an audio prompt.

Differentiation: Suggest that more confident children segment and sound out the words for themselves.

Creature cards

- Ask children to suggest different creatures that could be found in Juba's vegetable plot (for example, a snail, a chicken, a bee, an ant, a worm or a goat) and write out these creatures' names.
- Ask the children to sound out, blend and read out each word, and then to draw a small image card for animal.
- Write out word cards to match, and ask groups to match the word cards with the correct pictures.

Differentiation: More confident children may be able to help you to create the word cards.

Beanstalk sentences

- Cut out copies of the image and sentence cards from Resource Sheet 9.1 and give one full set to each pair of talk partners.
- Help or guide the children to read out part or all of the simple sentences, using reading cues such as segmenting, blending, syllables and prediction to help them.
- Once they have read the sentences, ask the children to match them to the correct pictures.

Differentiation: Give extra support to less confident children by asking them to look at the pictures as cues and sound out taught phonemes. Offer support with reading the sentences, as required.

Writing

The top of the beanstalk

- Tell the children the fairy tale, 'Jack and the Beanstalk'. At the end, ask them what Jack finds at the top of his magic beanstalk. Write and read out the sentence 'Jack finds a giant.'
- Ask the children what they would like to find at the top of the beanstalk.
- Ask the children to write their own sentences using that model (for example, 'Ali finds a king.').
- Ask them to draw pictures to go with their sentences.

Differentiation: Encourage more confident writers to write whole sentences, with help offered for the tricky parts of words (such as 'alien' or 'dinosaur'). Write out the sentences for less confident writers, leaving a gap for them to write their names and the initial letters of the remaining words. Less confident writers should orally compose their sentences; record these and guide them in the segmentation of accessible words used in their sentence.

Bean words

- Ask mixed-ability pairs to complete the interactive activity 'Bean Words', dragging letters into their correct places to label pictures after an audio prompt.

Phonics Work

The snail game

- Give mixed-ability pairs Resource Sheet 9.2, counters and a 1–4 spinner.
- When a child reaches a segment of the shell, they sound, segment and blend the word on that segment to find out what it is.
- The first child to the middle wins the game, but only if they can then use their 'ai' words to make verbal sentences.

Differentiation: More confident children could write out their 'ai' sentences, or perhaps make their own snail games, using other words with a common phoneme.

Juba's scarecrow

- Ask mixed-ability pairs to complete the interactive activity 'Juba's Scarecrow', dragging the correct label to the scarecrow outline.

Differentiation: Encourage less confident children to focus on the taught phonemes of the labels.

CROSS-CURRICULAR ACTIVITIES

Adult-led activities 👥

Growing beanstalks (Understanding the World)

Work with the children to start growing beanstalks:

- Ask the children to place their beans on wet cotton wool in a glass jar.
- Place the jars by a good light source.
- Encourage the children to look at their bean jars often, to check on growth and water.

Bean games (Physical Development)

- Use bean bags for a range of physical activities to encourage coordination and cooperative play (for example, throwing and catching, throwing at a target or balancing).

Beanstalk displays (Expressive Arts)

- Create a display for the class to show the different stages of the growth of a bean to a beanstalk. Ask the children to add in written labels and drawings to go with it.
- 3D beanstalk models could be made using five sheets of newspaper tightly rolled up together and cut a third of the way down; pull upwards from the middle for the beanstalk to grow. A soft version could be made from newspaper or cloth stuffed into green tights.

Beans for meals (Understanding the World; PSHE)

- Bring in a range of different beans for the children to examine in more detail.
- Suggest various ways the children can explore and compare the differences between the beans (for example, their sizes, shapes, textures, colours, names and, if cooked, tastes).
- Encourage the children to talk about their favourite bean dishes, such as bean stew.
- Create a bean stew for the children to taste.

Child-led activities 👥 👥

Bean shakers (Expressive Arts)

- Suggest that the children make bean percussion instruments by putting dried beans into plastic bottles to form shakers (a little like maracas).
- Let them experiment with how many beans they use – do they make different sounds?

Beanstalk corner (Communication and Language)

- Set up a beanstalk-themed corner, including a 3D beanstalk, for imaginary play.
- 3D beanstalk models could be made using five sheets of newspaper tightly rolled up together and cut a third of the way down; pull upwards from the middle for the beanstalk to grow. A soft version could be made from newspaper or cloth stuffed into green tights.
- Children can use this corner to look at a variety of books on beans as well as copies of 'Jack and the Beanstalk' and 'Juba's Bean'.

Bean hunting (PSHE; Mathematics)

- Hide a set number of dried beans and ask pairs of children to find and count them out.
- Ask the children to hide the beans for others to find, too.

SEQUENCE ASSESSMENT

Communication and Language

- Does the child join in with repeated refrains and anticipates key events and phrases in rhymes and stories?
- Does the child focus attention – still listen or do, but shifts own attention?
- Does the child listen and respond to ideas expressed by others in conversation or discussion?
- Does the child show evidence of extending their vocabulary?
- Does the child use intonation, rhythm and phrasing to make the meaning clear to others?
- Does the child use talk to organise, sequence and clarify thinking, ideas, feelings and events?

Reading

- Can the child recognise rhythm in spoken words?
- Can the child listen to and join in with stories and poems, one-to-one and also in small groups?
- Can the child join in with repeated refrains?
- Can the child anticipate key events and phrases in rhymes and stories?
- Can the child show interest in illustrations and print in books and print in the environment?
- Can the child hear and say the initial sounds in CVC, CVCC and CCVC words?
- Can the child segment the sounds in simple words and blend them together?
- Can the child recognise and use the sound for 'ai' when blending words together?
- Can the child begin to read words and simple sentences?

Writing

- Can the child continue a rhyming string?
- Can the child segment and blend sounds for words relating to the story and write them down?
- Can the child recognise and write down initial letters in CVC/CVCC/CCVC words?
- Can the child segment, blend and write words that contain the phoneme/ai/?
- Can the child write short sentences?

Review of the Big Picture

At the end of this sequence, discuss with the children what they liked about the rhyme, 'Juba's Bean'. Ask: *What are the days of the week? What did Juba do on the different days? What has she learnt about growing beans? What have you learnt about beans? What new words did you learn to read and write?*

Encourage each child to show and explain examples of their writing and reading achievements, and any cross-curricular activities they enjoyed.

Use the 'Pupil observation chart' to record each child's responses and attainment.

SEQUENCE 10 Animals: Birds

TERM 2 (SPRING): 2nd half term

Main Topic:	Animals
Subtopic:	Birds
Text Type:	Story
Main Source Text:	*Henny Penny* by Vivian French and Sophie Windham (ISBN 978-0-747-58104-8)
Extra Source Text:	*Chicken Licken* by Mandy Ross (ISBN 978-1-409-30956-7)
Approximate Duration:	Two weeks

Big Picture

During this sequence, children will hear about the original story of 'Chicken Licken', and then listen to a version with a different ending: 'Henny Penny'. They will discuss its sequence, characters, repetitive phrases and rhyming vocabulary as a group.
A range of supportive activities will also give the children an opportunity to explore the story and characters in more detail.

Phonics Focuses

The children will practise hearing and saying sounds for letters, and segment and blend the phonemes for the graphemes 'ck' and 'ng' in CVC and CVCC words. They will also explore rhyming words and spelling patterns.
Learning Outcomes: See 'Learning Outcomes' Chart, on pages xi–xiv.
Key Vocabulary: Henny Penny, acorn, sky, king, sensible, terrible, hearth

Home Links

Encourage children to:
- have a parent or carer read other versions of the Chicken Licken story
- find out more about farm animals, including hens, ducks, geese, turkeys and cockerels (and about foxes)
- listen to other traditional stories with similar chain-like structures, such as 'The Gingerbread Man'.

Resources Required

Workbook Pages: 12, 19–20
Resource Sheets 10.1–10.2: Story Puppets; Sequencing 'Henny Penny'

General Resources:
- Craft materials (e.g. lollipop sticks, straws, coloured feathers, felt, furry fabric, newspaper, tape, glue, paint)
- String
- Pegs
- Craft paper
- Dusters (and other basic cleaning supplies)

Background Knowledge

Explain to the children that:
- the original story of Chicken Licken is very old: it was written down by the Grimm brothers in the early 1800s
- in 'Chicken Licken', the main character believes the sky is falling (down) and rushes to tell the king, meeting friends and then a fox along the way
- it is a good example of a 'chain' story: a basic action is repeated and built up through the story to a final conclusion, and includes repetitive language
- the main repeated phrase in this story is usually 'The sky is falling (down)!'
- in most versions, Chicken Licken (or Henny Penny) and her friends are lured to a fox's den and eaten before they can reach the king – or just one character escapes to see the king
- the story also has a moral: not to believe everything you hear!

Performance Ideas and Storytelling Suggestions

- ⭐ Read the story out loud to yourself before reading it to the class, to help you decide where you could add emphasis and intonation to key words or lines (for example, by using different voices, actions and facial expressions, for the different characters).
- ⭐ Say the repetitive phrases slowly so the children can join in. Pause just before saying 'the sky fell down', so that the children can say it too. The main repetitive text occurs when Henny Penny meets a new animal (until she meets Foxy Loxy). It is:

She/They hadn't gone far when she/they met [animal's name].
'You look to be in a terrible hurry. Where are you going?'
'I was shaking my duster this way and that way round and round, and all of a sudden the sky fell down! And I don't know what to do, so I'm/we're going to tell the king.'
'If the sky is falling down, I'd better come with you.'
So [animals' names] pit-pit-pattered along the road together.

Sequence Structure

This chart offers suggestions on the order and timings of exploring the story over a two-week period. However, please feel free to adapt the sessions to your own planning and suitable timings for your whole class or set groups.

Exploring the Story

Tip: If possible, aim to read or show the story to the children regularly over the two-week period, or before any related activity, so that the children get to know the story and its messages well.

WEEK 1 (PHASE 1)	WEEKS 1–2 (PHASE 2)	WEEKS 1–2 (PHASE 3)
Introduction to the story	**Getting to know the story**	**Performing the story**
All sections could be done in one session or split over two or three sessions.	Aim to hold one or two sessions on getting to know the story, each retelling the story and then including your own choice of activities.	Aim to hold one or two sessions at different times across the two-week period.
1. **What do we know?** (approx. 20 minutes) 2. **Let's listen and talk** (approx. 20 minutes) **Extra consolidation activity:** • Characters and their noises (approx. 20 minutes)	3. **Let's get to know the story** (10–15 minutes) **'Structure focus' activities:** • Sequencing 'Henny Penny' (20–25 minutes) • The big surprises (approx. 15 minutes) **'Vocabulary focus' activity:** • Henny Penny's lullaby (approx. 20 minutes) **'Phonics focus' activity:** • 'ck' words (approx. 15 minutes)	4. **Let's put on a performance** (30–40 minutes)

Literacy Activities

READING	WRITING	PHONICS WORK
• Henny Penny's animals • Rhyming names	• Group chain story • Trips to the king	• What's in Foxy Loxy's den? • Walking sounds

Cross-curricular Activities

Adult-led activities:	Child-led activities:
• Character puppets (Communication and Language; Expressive Arts) • Rhyming names (Communication and Language) • Henny Penny games (Physical Development; Communication and Language)	• Collage characters (Expressive Arts) • Henny Penny maths (Mathematics) • Cleaning the den (PSHE; Communication and Language) • Animal information (Understanding the World; PSHE)

Sequence Assessment

• Communication and Language
• Reading
• Writing
• Review of the Big Picture

EXPLORING THE STORY

PHASE 1: Introduction to the story

Session 1: What do we know?

Before the session, prepare the story puppets from Resource Sheet 10.1 by cutting out the characters and attaching then to pencils, lollipop sticks or straws.

Discuss the **Background Knowledge** given above, and ask questions to ascertain children's knowledge of the traditional tale 'Chicken Licken'.

Then show the children the Henny Penny puppet. Introduce the character to the children, and note

that 'Henny' rhymes with 'Penny': it ends with the same sounds.

Explain that you have heard of a story about Henny Penny that ends differently from 'Chicken Licken'. Ask the children how they think this new story might end. Then explain that they are going to listen to this new story and do lots of fun activities connected with it.

Session 2: Let's listen and talk

Show the children the Henny Penny puppet again, and remind them briefly of their discussion about the old and new versions of 'Chicken Licken' and 'Henny Penny'. Explain that they are going to listen to the new version.

Show the **Storyteller** video for 'Henny Penny' on **Connect**, or read the story yourself (see the **Performance Ideas and Storytelling Suggestions** above).

After the reading, check that the children understand any new or difficult words (see **Key Vocabulary** above).

Ask questions to check the children's understanding of the story. These can be open to group discussion or children can pair with talk partners before reporting back to the group. For example:

- *Why did Henny Penny think the sky was falling down?*
- *Who is Henny Penny going to tell?*

- *Where does Foxy Loxy lead Henny Penny and her friends?*
- *What is Foxy Loxy's den like?*
- *What does Foxy Loxy plan to have for dinner?*
- *How does Henny Penny trick Foxy Loxy?*
- *What do Henny Penny and her friends enjoy at the end of the day?*

Finally, discuss the moral of the story (not to believe everything you hear), and how it fits with the story's events.

Extra consolidation activity

Characters and their noises

- Show the story puppets made from Resource Sheet 10.1.
- Hold up each one in turn (Henny Penny, Ducky Lucky, Cocky Locky, Goosey Loosey and then Turkey Lurkey), and ask the children what the character is called.
- Then ask them to make the appropriate animal sound, as used in the story ('cluck cluck cluck', 'quack quack quack', 'cock-a-doodle-doo', 'hiss hiss hiss' or 'gobble gobble gobble').
- Finally, hold up the Foxy Loxy puppet and ask the children to decide, as a group, what noise he would make.
- Then put the children into six different groups and allocate each group a character.
- In story order, ask the bird groups to say, 'The sky is falling down!' followed by their animal noise. Ask the fox group to say, 'Come for dinner!' followed by their noise.

EXPLORING THE STORY

PHASE 2: Getting to know the story

Session 3: Let's get to know the story 👥 👥

Show the children the Henny Penny puppet again, and remind them of the story. Ask them what they remember about it. Retell the story using the **Storyteller** video on **Connect**, or read the story yourself. Encourage the children to join in with the animal noises and the repetitive phrases they can remember (for example, 'the sky fell down!').

After the retelling, choose focus activities to explore the story in more depth.

'Structure focus' activities

Sequencing 'Henny Penny' 👥 👥

- Hang a line of string across a display board.
- Cut out the images from Resource Sheet 10.2 and display them in a mixed-up order.
- Ask the children where the story started, and to find the image that shows this.
- Ask a child to attach this image to the line.
- Prompt the children to continue retelling the story, and adding images to the line until they reach Henny Penny's cottage again.

The big surprises 👥 👥

- Display the interactive activity 'The Big Surprises'.
- Ask the children to look at the images of surprises that could have featured in the story, and to discuss if that surprise was in the story.
- Ask the children to instruct you in dragging the correct images into the correct order.
- Discuss why these were surprises for the characters.

'Vocabulary focus' activity

Henny Penny's lullaby 👥 👥

- Display the interactive activity 'Henny Penny's Lullaby'.
- Read out the first two lines, and ask the children to whom and why Henny Penny sang them.
- Note that the words 'eyes' and 'surprise' rhyme.
- Read the lines of the other verses, and ask the children to choose the correct missing rhyme from the three possibilities supplied.
- Then read out the completed lullaby to the children, encouraging them to join in with the rhyming words.

'Phonics focus' activity

'ck' words 👥 👥

- Show the puppet of Ducky Lucky.
- Write out the word 'duck', underline the 'ck' and ask the children to make the/k/sound.
- Point to each grapheme as you sound and blend the word.
- Write and ask the children to sound out other 'ck' words (for example, 'quack', 'luck' and 'cluck').
- Encourage the children to think of other words that contain 'ck', to add to the list.

EXPLORING THE STORY

PHASE 3: Performing the story

Session 4: Let's put on a performance

Over the two weeks, encourage the children to explore the story through role-play. For example:

- Hold a movement session in which the children pretend to be the different animals in the story. Ask them to work on how each animal would move and sound both when relaxed and when panicked. They could change their behaviour when you shout, 'The sky is falling down!'

During the final session, remind the children of their work so far. Show the story again using the **Storyteller** video on **Connect**, or retell it with the children from the whiteboard. Then ask the children to work together to act out the story.

- Put the children into six groups, one for each story character (Henny Penny, Ducky Lucky, Cocky Locky, Goosey Loosey, Turkey Lurkey and Foxy Loxy).
- Remind them of how their characters move, and the noises they make.
- Place the groups in different parts of the room, in story order.
- Read out the story and ask the children to act out their roles once they are reached.
- Start at the Henny Penny group, encouraging the children to stand up and mime the actions. Then have one child lead the way to the next group, with the rest of the group following in a line behind them.
- Continue until all the groups are together (once you reach Foxy Loxy's den).
- Ask the children to stay in character and mime their actions until the bird groups run home.

LITERACY ACTIVITIES

Reading

Henny Penny's animals

- Ask mixed-ability pairs to work on the interactive activity 'Henny Penny's Animals', dragging the correct word to each animal image after an audio prompt.

Differentiation: Encourage more confident readers to compose sentences orally using the words given.

Rhyming names

- Create a set of 12 word cards, each containing one word from the list of character names (for example, a card saying 'Cocky' and another saying 'Locky'). Write the initial letter of each name in a different colour, underline it or make it bolder.
- Lay out the first-name cards and the last-name cards separately.
- Ask a child to choose a first name and then to match it to its rhyming last name, asking them to look for matching letter patterns at the ends of the words.

Differentiation: Assist less confident children by offering an audio prompt for a word if they point at it.

Writing

Group chain story

- Show images of animals with CVC or CVCC names (for example, a hen, a dog, a cat, a rat, a duck and a fox).
- With the children, sound out and segment the animal names, and then write them under the images.
- Tell the children that the animals are going to see the king.
- Ask the class to suggest why they are going there, and how their journey will end.
- Write a simple story start (for example, 'The hen thinks the sun is going out, so it runs to the king.')
- Allocate the different animals to different groups/pairs of children and ask them to write this simple sentence: 'The [animal name] runs to the king.'
- Then ask them to draw a picture to illustrate their sentence.
- Display their work after your story starter, and add an ending to complete the chain story (for example, 'The king thinks the sun is not going out.').

Differentiation: Write out the sentence, leaving a gap for the animal name, for less confident writers to spell using taught phonemes.

Trips to the king

- Ask mixed-ability pairs to work on the interactive activity 'A Trip to the King', following the different paths to three graphemes and dragging them into order to make the word 'king'.

Differentiation: Ask more confident writers to write down more words ending in –ing (for example, 'sing', 'ring' or 'wing').

Phonics Work

What's in Foxy Loxy's den?

- Ask mixed-ability pairs to work on the interactive activity 'What's in Foxy Loxy's Den?', dragging six labels to their matching objects. (There is an audio prompt, but ask the children to try to sound out and blend each object word first.)

Differentiation: Ask more confident children to find more objects in the image and write labels for them.

Walking sounds

- Look back at the story and note that the birds 'pit-pit-pattered' along the road.
- Look at other spelling pattern words that could be used for similar walking actions, such as 'hip-hip-hopped' or 'tip-tip-tapped'.

CROSS-CURRICULAR ACTIVITIES

Adult-led activities 👥👤

Character puppets (Communication and Language; Expressive Arts)

- Cut out more of the character puppets from Resource Sheet 10.1.
- Ask the children to decorate the puppets, or to copy them to create their own.
- Encourage groups to retell the story, using their puppets to act it out.

Rhyming names (Communication and Language)

- Remind the children about how the characters' names rhyme.
- Ask them to come up with an extra rhyming part for their own names, and to discuss these with talk partners. (Make sure the rhyming names are not too personal or offensive!)
- Write out the names and ask the children to copy them down and decorate them, or to use the computer to create an effective text design.

Henny Penny games (Physical Development; Communication and Language)

Play a set of games that can be linked to the story. Ideas include:

- Following Henny Penny: the children follow a leader through an obstacle course, being guided by directional language such as 'under', 'around', 'over', 'right' and 'left'.
- The Birds' Footsteps: The children have to creep up to and pass the 'fox' without being heard.
- 'Fox and Goose' circle game and 'What's the time, Mr Fox?' chasing game.

Child-led activities 👥👤 👥 👤

Collage characters (Expressive Arts)

- Draw outlines of the bird characters onto craft paper.
- Ask the children to stick craft materials onto the images to make textural collages, such as coloured feathers, felt and furry material.
- Offer images of the animals to help them with their choices if necessary.
- Encourage the children to feel and describe the textures as they create them.

Henny Penny maths (Mathematics)

- Ask children to count the story characters as they remember the story sequence.
- Set a task, such as planning a tea party, and ask the children to work out how many plates, cups or pieces of cutlery they will need.

Differentiation: Ask more confident children to add animals to the story and then repeat the activity.

Cleaning the den (PSHE; Communication and Language)

- Create a messy 'fox's den' role-play area, with some labelled empty boxes where certain items could be put away. Make available some basic cleaning supplies, such as dusters.
- Explain that, to escape the fox, the birds first had to clean his den.
- Ask groups to tidy and clean the area, putting away objects and clearing surfaces.

Animal information (Understanding the World; PSHE)

- Allocate the different animals in the story to different groups.
- Challenge the groups to find out more about their animals using books the internet and their own experiences, and to present what they learn simply.

SEQUENCE ASSESSMENT

Communication and Language
- Does the child listen to the story with increasing attention and recall?
- Does the child anticipate key events in the story?
- Does the child listen and respond to ideas expressed by others in conversation or discussion?
- Does the child use talk to organise, sequence and clarify thinking and ideas about the story?
- Does the child show evidence of extending their vocabulary?
- Does the child introduce and explore the story in their play?

Reading
- Is the child aware of how the story is structured?
- Can the child describe the main story setting, events and characters?
- Can the child hear and say the initial sounds in words?
- Can the child segment the sounds in simple words and blend them together?
- Can the child begin to read words and simple sentences?
- Can the child use vocabulary and forms of speech that are increasingly influenced by traditional tales?

Writing
- Can the child continue a rhyming string?
- Can the child blend sounds for words and write them down?
- Can the child recognise initial sounds for letters in words?
- Can the child write their own name and simple labels and captions?
- Can the child attempt to write short sentences for a short story?

Review of the Big Picture

At the end of this sequence, discuss with the children what they liked about the story 'Henny Penny'. Ask: *In what order did the animals appear in the story? How did the birds escape the fox? What phrases or words did you like most? Which was your favourite rhyming word?*

Encourage each child to show and explain examples of their writing and reading achievements, and any cross-curricular activities they enjoyed.

Use the 'Pupil observation chart' to record each child's responses and attainment.

SEQUENCE 11 Animals: Bees

TERM 2 (SPRING) 2nd half term

Main Topic:	Animals
Subtopic:	Bees
Text Type:	Poem
Main Source Text:	'Watching a Bumble-Bee', from *Here Come the Creatures* by Wes Magee (ISBN 978-1-847-80367-2)
Approximate Duration:	Two weeks

Big Picture

During this sequence, children will listen to the poem 'Watching a Bumble-Bee' and discuss the poem's subject, vocabulary and repetitive, rhyming structure as a group.

Through a range of supportive activities, the children will have the opportunity to explore bees and their behaviour in more depth.

Phonics Focuses

The children will practise hearing and saying sounds for letters, and segment and blend the phonemes for the graphemes 'z' and 'zz', as well as 'ee'. They will also explore rhyming spelling patterns for CVC and CVCC words.

Learning Outcomes: See 'Learning Outcomes' Chart, on pages xi–xiv.

Key Vocabulary: bumblebee, vest, nectar, honey, tizz

Home Links

Encourage children to:

- find out more about bees
- find out more about other garden insects, such as ants, ladybirds and beetles
- keep an eye out for bees and other insects
- find out more about honey and how it is used.

Resources Required

Workbook Pages: 17–19, 21–22

Resource Sheets 11.1–11.3: Bee Finger Puppets; Honeycomb Templates; Bee Rhymes

General Resources:

- An image of a bee
- A jar of honey
- Yellow counters
- Craft paper
- Craft materials (e.g. pens, paint, cloth, newspaper, tape, glue, pipe cleaners)
- Ingredients for honey sweets (honey, peanut butter and vanilla essence)
- Mixing bowls
- Wooden spoons
- Thread
- Coat hangers

Background Knowledge

Explain to the children that:

- the five short verses in the poem describe where the bee is, what it looks like, what it is doing, what it sounds like and how it moves
- bees are a kind of flying insect with black and yellow stripes
- bees live in large groups with other bees
- bees play an important role in helping plants to survive (by spreading their pollen)
- bees sting only if they are threatened
- bees make honey. (The poem is about a bumble-bee, but the bee that traditionally collects nectar to make honey is the honey bee.)

Performance Ideas and Storytelling Suggestions

- ★ Read through the poem out loud to yourself before performing it to the class, to help you decide where to add emphasis and intonation to key words or lines (for example, by emphasising the rhyming words).
- ★ Read the 'oh-so-' phrases slowly so the children can hear them.
- ★ Use hand actions (see the 'Watching a Bumble-Bee' text on **Connect**). Practise and learn these before performing them to the children.
- ★ Make a loud 'zz' sound following the last word, and gradually tail it off as if the bee is flying away.

Sequence Structure

This chart offers suggestions on the order and timings of exploring the story over a two-week period. However, please feel free to adapt the sessions to your own planning and suitable timings for your whole class or set groups.

Exploring the Poem

Tip: If possible, aim to perform the poem to or with the children regularly over the two-week period, or before any related activity, so that the children get to know the poem and its meaning well.

WEEK 1 (PHASE 1)	WEEKS 1–2 (PHASE 2)	WEEK 2 (PHASE 3)
Introduction to the poem	**Getting to know the poem**	**Performing the poem**
All sections could be done in one session or split over two or three sessions.	Aim to hold one or two sessions on getting to know the poem, each retelling the poem and then including your own choice of activities.	These sessions could be rehearsed and performed at different times across the week.
1. **What do we know?** (15–20 minutes) 2. **Let's listen and talk** (approx. 30 minutes) **Extra consolidation activity:** ● Bee finger puppets (30–45 minutes)	3. **Let's get to know the poem** (10–15 minutes) **'Structure focus' activities:** ● What the poem tells us (approx. 20 minutes) ● 'Oh-so-busy' repetitive phrases (approx. 20 minutes) **'Vocabulary focus' activity:** ● A bee display (approx. 20 minutes) **'Phonics focus' activity:** ● Rhyming flower (15–20 minutes)	4. **Let's put on a performance** (30–40 minutes)

Literacy Activities

READING	WRITING	PHONICS WORK
● Beehive words ● Honeycomb words	● 'B' words ● Bee sentences	● Buzzy words ● Buzzy syllables

Cross-curricular Activities

Adult-led activities:	Child-led activities:
● Bee rhymes (Expressive Arts; Communication and Language) ● Honey sweets (Expressive Arts; Understanding the World) ● Bee knowledge (Understanding the World)	● Flying bees (Expressive Arts) ● Busy bees (PSHE) ● Honeycomb shapes (Mathematics) ● Bee 'waggle' dances (Physical Education; Communication and Language)

Sequence Assessment

● Communication and Language
● Reading
● Writing
● Review of the Big Picture

EXPLORING THE POEM

PHASE 1: Introduction to the poem

Session 1: What do we know?

Show the children an image of a bee. Then give prompts and ask open questions to assess the children's current knowledge about bees. For example:

- *What is this?*
- *Where can we often see bees?*
- *What noise do bees make?*
- *Let's make a buzzing sound together.*
- *Has anyone ever been stung by a bee?*

Discuss the **Background Knowledge** given above. Show the children a jar of honey and allow them to taste it. Ask them to share their thoughts about its texture, taste and appearance.

Then explain to the children that they are going to find out more about bees by listening to a poem and doing lots of fun activities about them.

Session 2: Let's listen and talk

Introduce the poem 'Watching a Bumble-Bee' by showing the picture of a bee again. Remind the children briefly of their discussion about bees.

Show the **Storyteller** video for 'Watching a Bumble-Bee' on **Connect**, or display the poem and read it aloud. If you are performing the poem, use the poem text on **Connect** for hints and directions, and include props and/or images, if required (see also the **Performance Ideas and Storytelling Suggestions** above).

After the reading, check that the children understand any new or difficult words (see **Key Vocabulary** above).

Ask questions to check the children's understanding of the poem. These can be open to group discussion or children can pair with talk partners before reporting back to the group. For example:

- *How are bees different from human beings?*
- *Would you rather be a bee or a human being?*

- *Where does the poem say you can see the bumble bee?*
- *What is its 'vest' like?*
- *What is the bee gathering?*
- *What is the bee humming?*
- *What can the bee make that is sweet?*
- *How does it move about?*
- *What sound does the bee make?*

Say the poem one more time. Let the children join in with the actions and the 'zz' sound of the last word. (After the extra consolidation activity, if completed, ask the children to use their puppets while you retell the poem again.)

Extra consolidation activity

Bee finger puppets

- Show the image of the bee again.
- Ask the children to describe its colours and how they think a bee might feel. (Ensure that the children know they should not try to touch a bee in real life.)
- Cut out a bee puppet for each child using Resource Sheet 11.1.
- Ask each child to colour in and decorate their puppet using any craft materials available.
- Encourage the children to play, putting their puppets on their fingers and making buzzing sounds.
- Let the children use their puppets whenever the poem is being retold.

EXPLORING THE POEM

PHASE 2: Getting to know the poem

Session 3: Let's get to know the poem 👥 👥

Show the children the picture of the bee again, and remind them of the poem. Ask them what they remember about it. Retell the poem using the **Storyteller** video on **Connect**, or by displaying the poem and reading it aloud to the class. Then retell the poem again, asking the children to join in with the last two words in the second line of each verse (and using their bee puppets, if made).

After the retelling, choose focus activities to explore the poem in more depth.

'Structure focus' activities

What the poem tells us 👥 👥

- Explain to the children that the poem tells us five things about the bee – where it is, what it looks like, what it does, what it sounds like, and how it moves.
- Discuss each one in more detail with the children, as well as encouraging them to share their own knowledge about bees.

'Oh-so-busy' repetitive phrases 👥 👥

- Display the interactive activity 'Oh-so-busy'.
- Read the first verse and then note that, in the later verses, the describing phrases are missing.
- Ask the children if they remember what these could be, before clicking on the drop-down menu to show three possible answers.
- Read them out and ask the children to decide which is correct. (If necessary, read the whole verse with each word choice, to help them work out which makes sense.)
- Repeat these steps for the remaining verses but, in the final verse, ask the children to work out the last action word.

Differentiation: More confident children could suggest different descriptive phrases to be added in (for example, 'oh-so-stripy'/'oh-so-friendly').

'Vocabulary focus' activity

A bee display 👥 👥

- Use a craft session to create a garden scene featuring bees, flowers, a tree with a bees nest and a beehive.
- Show the children some pre-prepared word labels for the things featured in the garden (for example, 'flowers', 'tree', 'hive' and 'bees').
- Point to a feature that needs a label, and ask the children what label you should use. Ask the children to sound the labels' initial letters, to help them to work out which is correct.
- Add the labels to the display.
- (More images and labels could be added during the week (for example, a beekeeper, a honeycomb).

'Phonics focus' activity

Rhyming flower 👥 👥

- Say the poem's second verse, putting emphasis on the rhyming words, for example, rest – vest.
- Ask the children which two words rhyme.
- Display the interactive activity 'Rhyming Flower'.
- Look at the flower and say the word in the top petal: 'vest'. Sound out and blend the last three letters with the children.
- Look at the mix of words under the flower.
- Ask the children to listen to each word and decide which ones rhyme with 'vest'.
- Drag these words into the petals.
- When the activity is complete, read through each '–est' word with the children so they can hear the rhyming spelling pattern again.
- Then sound out and blend each word.

EXPLORING THE POEM

PHASE 3: Performing the poem

Session 4: Let's put on a performance 👥 👥

Over the week, encourage the children to explore the poem through role-play by asking them to move, sound and behave like bees in different moods:

- Happy, relaxed bees, flying off to search for a garden full of flowers – encourage the children to use their wings and bodies to convey a gentle swaying movement, and to buzz or hum quietly.

- Excited bees that are 'in a tizz' in the garden, going from flower to flower, buzzing and moving about busily.

- Bees with heavy loads of nectar, flying home in a zigzag fashion with a 'buzzy whizz'.

During the final session, remind the children of their work so far. Show the poem again using the **Storyteller** video on **Connect**, or retell it with the children from the whiteboard. Then ask the children to work together to create a performance of the poem.

- Allocate each group of children sets of two rhyming lines to perform.

- Ask each group to prepare a presentation of their lines, using role-play (as explored over the week) and memorising the rhyming words at the ends of the two lines.

- Ask the groups to stand in order, and then – as you read out the poem – to join in with their performances or presentations at the appropriate time.

- Encourage all children to make a long buzzing noise at the end when the final word, 'whizz', is read out.

- If possible, film the performance for the children to watch and enjoy.

Differentiation: More confident readers may wish to read their lines along with their performances or assist you in reading out the poem.

LITERACY ACTIVITIES

Reading

Beehive words

- Ask mixed-ability pairs to work on the interactive activity 'Beehive Words', listening to three simple sentences with missing words and then dragging the correct words from the hive.

Differentiation: Encourage more confident readers to sound out and decode words instead of listening to the audio first. Ask them to compose their own sentences using the words orally.

Honeycomb words

- Write any sight words that the children find difficult or tricky words into the section of the honeycomb on Resource Sheet 11.2.
- Give the honeycomb board and a yellow 'bee' counter to a child (or pair of children).
- Say one of the words, and ask the child to find the word, read it back to you and then to cover it with the bee counter.
- If focusing on tricky words, encourage the children to note letters with familiar phonic sounds and letters that are tricky.

Writing

'B' words

- Work with the children to create a list of 10 CVC or CVCC words that start with 'b'. Aim for two words per vowel (for example, 'bag', 'back', 'bet', 'beg', 'bin', 'big', 'bog', 'boss', 'bug', 'bus').
- If children struggle, write out two consonants and ask them to suggest which vowel could make them into a word.
- Once the list is completed, ask the children to write the words out, underlining the vowels or writing them in a different colour.
- Attach string to the words and hang them from large 'B' shapes to create hanging mobiles.

Differentiation: Encourage more confident writers to create their own lists independently.

Bee sentences

- Ask mixed-ability pairs to work on the interactive activity 'Bee Sentences', dragging the words into place to create a sentence after an audio prompt.

Differentiation: Ask more confident writers to use the words to write their own sentences, composing these orally first.

Phonics Work

Buzzy words

- Ask mixed-ability pairs to work on the interactive activity 'Buzzy Words', selecting the words that contain 'zz'.

Differentiation: Ask more confident children think of more words containing 'zz' or 'z'.

Buzzy syllables

- Ask the children to sit in a circle.
- Say any one-or two-syllable words, and ask the children to clap the syllables.
- Once they are comfortable with hearing syllables, change the claps to the words 'bizz', for one syllable, and 'bizz, buzz' for two syllables. For example: 'ant': 'bizz'. 'garden': 'bizz, buzz'.

CROSS-CURRICULAR ACTIVITIES

Adult-led activities

Bee rhymes (Expressive Arts; Communication and Language)

- Allocate each of the three rhymes on Resource Sheet 11.3 to a group.
- Work with the groups to prepare simple performances of the rhymes, using expressive actions.
- Ask the groups to perform their rhymes for one another.

Honey food (Expressive Arts; Understanding the World)

- Try out simple recipes such as honey biscuits or honey cake for the children to bake.
- Find out more about world foods/recipes that use honey such as baklava.
- Invite in a parent or carer who may use honey in their cooking to share their knowledge.

NB: Check dietary warnings for individual children before you try a tasting session.

Bee knowledge (Understanding the World)

- Show a short, simple documentary about bees so the children can find out more about pollination and/or the honey-making process. (There are several available on popular video-sharing websites.)
- If possible, ask a local wildlife expert or beekeeper to come in and talk about bees.

Bee investigation – messy play (Communication and Language)

- Let the children investigate the feel, textures and colour of a range of different honeys.
- Put the honeys in different bowls for the children to put their hands into.
- Encourage them to discuss their findings or complete a tick sheet.

NB: Check dietary warnings for individual children before you try a tasting session.

Child-led activities

Flying bees (Expressive Arts)

- Ask the children to make small bees using a range of craft materials, for example, woollen pom pom bees, wooden spoon bees, pipe cleaner bees, soft dough or clay bees, or paper plate bees.
- Use thread to hang the bees from coat hangers and hang them from the classroom ceiling.

Busy bees (PSHE)

- Create a 'Busy bees' chart, allocating different areas of the classroom to different children at different times.
- At their allocated times, the children should become 'busy bees' and help to tidy up their areas.

Honeycomb shapes (Mathematics)

- Cut out the hexagons from Resource Sheet 11.2.
- Ask children to explore how they fit together, and to make different patterns.
- Cut out other simple shapes, such as squares and triangles, for the children to include too.

Bee 'waggle' dances (Physical Education; Communication and Language)

- Explain to the children that honeybees do a 'waggle' dance to tell other bees where flowers are.
- Encourage the children to create their own waggle dances, and then to follow each other around the room to an imaginary garden.
- Ensure that they share being the leader and followers.

SEQUENCE ASSESSMENT

Communication and Language
- Does the child listen and respond to discussion about the poem?
- Does the child join in with and recognise repeated refrains in the poem?
- Has the child extended their vocabulary by exploring the meanings and sounds of new words?
- Does the child use talk to organise, sequence and clarify thinking and ideas about the poem?
- Does the child show evidence of extending their vocabulary?

Reading
- Can the child recognise rhythm in the poem's verses?
- Can the child anticipate key words and rhymes in the poem?
- Can the child hear initial sounds for words?
- Can the child segment and blend sounds in CVC/CVCC words?
- Can the child recognise the sound /z/ spelt 'z' and 'zz'?
- Can the child read simple sentences?

Writing
- Can the child segment and blend sounds in CVC/CVCC words?
- Can the child use some clearly identifiable letters to communicate meaning, representing some sounds correctly and in sequence?
- Can the child begin to write labels and words for captions?

Review of the Big Picture
At the end of this sequence, discuss with the children what they liked about 'Watching a Bumble-Bee'. Ask: *Which verse did you like most? What did you learn about bees? What 'zz' words did you enjoy saying?*

Encourage each child to show and explain examples of their writing and reading achievements, and any cross-curricular activities they enjoyed.

Use the 'Pupil observation chart' to record each child's responses and attainment.

SEQUENCE 12 Animals: Sea Creatures

TERM 2 (SPRING): 2nd half term

Main Topic:	Animals
Subtopic:	Sea Creatures
Text Type:	Story
Main Source Text:	*Sharing a Shell* by Julia Donaldson (ISBN 978-1-405-02048-0)
Extra Source Text:	*Commotion in the Ocean* by Giles Andreae (ISBN 978-1-841-21101-5)
Approximate Duration:	Two weeks

Big Picture

During this sequence, children will listen to the story 'Sharing a Shell' and discuss its settings, messages, characters, repetitive phrases and rhyming vocabulary as a group. They will also use the story to help develop skills in reading and writing words and simple sentences.

A range of supportive activities will give the children an opportunity to explore the story and its sea-creature characters in more detail.

Phonics Focuses

The children will practise hearing and saying phonemes, and segmenting and blending sounds for the graphemes 'th' and 'sh' in CVC, CVCC and CCVC words. They will also explore rhyming words, spelling patterns and tricky words.

Learning Outcomes: See 'Learning Outcomes' Chart, on pages xi–xiv.

Key Vocabulary: crab, roaming, anemone, tentacle, romping, bristleworm, rollicking, whelk

Home Links

Encourage children to:

- share something special with a friend or family member
- find out more about hermit crabs, anemones and bristleworms
- bring in any shells they may have, to show to the rest of the class.

Resources Required

Workbook Pages: 12, 15–16

Resource Sheet 12.1–12.3: Rock-pool Creatures; Word Shells; Tentacle 'th' Words

General Resources:

- A shell
- Kitchen foil
- Stones
- Craft materials (e.g. coloured pens and pencils, fabric, patterned/coloured paper, newspaper, tape, glue, paint, empty matchboxes, cardboard)
- Chalk
- Modelling dough
- Paper plates
- A range of shells and stones in different sizes and colours
- Water tubs
- Models of sea creatures
- Small, seaweed-like plants
- A large cardboard box

Background Knowledge

Explain to the children that:

- hermit crabs are a type of crab that has a soft body with no hard shell. This means they would be easy for other animals to eat
- hermit crabs find and curl their bodies inside empty shells that come from different shellfish. As they grow, they leave these shells to find bigger ones.
- 'Blob' is a sea anemone. Sea anemones look like plants but are actually animals. They can sting small creatures with their tentacles
- 'Brush' is a bristleworm. Bristleworms eat up dead things, so can keep shells and fish tanks clean.

Performance ideas and storytelling suggestions

- ★ Read through the story out loud to yourself before reading it to the class, to help you decide where you could add emphasis and intonation to key words or lines (for example, by using different voices, or using actions and facial expressions, for the different characters).
- ★ Emphasise the rhyming words in the text so the children can hear them clearly.
- ★ Say the repetitive phrases slowly so the children can hear them clearly and join in. Pause just before saying 'wonderful home for... [one/two/three], so the children can join in and anticipate the number.
- ★ Create different voices for each animal type, so that the children can work out who is speaking.

Sequence Structure

This chart offers suggestions on the order and timings of exploring the story over a two-week period. However, please feel free to adapt the sessions to your own planning and suitable timings for your whole class or set groups.

Exploring the Story

Tip: If possible, aim to read or show the story to the children regularly over the two-week period, or before any related activity, so that the children get to know the story and its messages well.

WEEK 1 (PHASE 1)	WEEKS 1–2 (PHASE 2)	WEEK 1–2 (PHASE 3)
Introduction to the story	**Getting to know the story**	**Exploring the story through role-play**
All sections could be done in one session or split over two or three sessions.	Aim to hold one or two sessions on getting to know the story, each retelling the story and then including your own choice of one or more activities.	Aim to hold one or two sessions at different times across the two-week period.
1. **What do we know?** (approx. 20 minutes) 2. **Let's listen and talk** (approx. 20 minutes) **Extra consolidation activity:** ● Sharing shells (approx. 20 minutes)	3. **Let's get to know the story** (10–15 minutes) **'Structure focus' activities:** ● Creatures in 'Sharing a Shell' (approx. 25 minutes) **'Vocabulary focus' activity:** ● Rock-pool rhyming words (approx. 20 minutes) ● A wonderful home (approx. 20 minutes) **'Phonics focus' activity:** ● Shell 'sh' words (approx. 15 minutes)	4. **Let's perform a role-play** ● **Crabby movements** (approx. 30 minutes) ● **Rollicking around the rock pool** (approx. 30 minutes)

Literacy Activities

READING	WRITING	PHONICS WORK
● Beach finds ● Word shells	● C is for crab ● Sea sentences	● Find the missing vowels ● Tentacle 'th' words

Cross-curricular Activities

Adult-led activities:
- A rock-pool display (Understanding the World; Expressive Arts)
- Shell spirals (Physical Development)
- Paper-plate shells (Expressive Arts)
- Sea stories (Communication and Language)

Child-led activities:
- Salt-dough characters (Expressive Arts)
- Shell sorting (Mathematics)
- Rock-pool tubs (Understanding the World; Communication and Language)
- Sharing a shell (Communication and Language; PSHE)

Sequence Assessment

- Communication and Language
- Reading
- Writing
- Review of the Big Picture

EXPLORING THE STORY

PHASE 1: Introduction to the story

Session 1: What do we know?

Show the children a shell. Explain that it came from a beach, near the sea, and was probably once the home of a sea creature. Then give prompts and ask open questions to assess the children's current knowledge about rock pools and sea creatures. For example:

- *Who has been to the beach and seen the sea?*
- *What kinds of animals and plants did you see?*
- *Did anyone see a rock pool?*
- *How is the water in a rock pool different from the sea itself?* (It is still.)
- *Has anyone ever seen a crab?*
- *How does a crab walk?* (sideways)

Discuss the **Background Knowledge** given above, and show the images from Resource Sheet 12.1. Point out the hermit crab in its different shells, the sea anemone, the bristleworm and the whelk.

Then explain to the children that they are going to listen to a story about a hermit crab, a sea anemone and a bristleworm who want to share a shell, and do lots of fun activities about sea creatures and the story.

Session 2: Let's listen and talk

Show the children the shell again, and remind them briefly of their discussion from the previous session.

Show the **Storyteller** video for 'Sharing a Shell' on **Connect**, or read the story yourself (see the **Performance Ideas and Storytelling Suggestions** above).

After the reading, check that the children understand any new or difficult words (see **Key Vocabulary** above).

Ask questions to check the children's understanding of the story. These can be open to group discussion or children can pair with talk partners before reporting back to the group. For example:

- *Who wanted to get into a shell?*
- *What did the crab do when he was chased by a gull?*

- *How did Blob the anemone scare the fish away?*
- *What was Brush the bristleworm good at doing?*
- *Where did the three friends like to play?*
- *Why did the crab and the anemone stop being friends?*
- *Who helped them to become friends again? How?*

Finally, ask the children to share their own experiences of sharing with friends, and how it made play more fun.

Extra consolidation activity

Sharing shells

- Ask the children to sit in a circle.
- Discuss how the crab in the story shared his shell with his friends, Blob and Brush.
- Ask the children to think of something special that they would each like to share with others (for example, a toy, game or day trip).
- Hold the shell and give a personal example.
- Pass the shell to the next child and ask them to give their suggestion.
- Continue this process around the circle.
- Finally, ask the children why they think the crab was sad when he stopped sharing with his friends. Discuss the ways in which sharing with friends and others is a good thing.

EXPLORING THE STORY

PHASE 2: Getting to know the story

Session 3: Let's get to know the story 👥 👥

Show the children the shell again, and remind them of the story. Ask them what they remember about it. Retell the story using the **Storyteller** video on **Connect**, or by reading it aloud to the class again yourself.

After the retelling, choose focus activities to explore the story in more depth.

'Structure focus' activity

Creatures in 'Sharing a Shell' 👥 👥

- Display the interactive activity 'Creatures in Sharing a Shell'.
- Look at the ten different shells on the screen.
- Explain to the children that, as a group, they need to find five sea creatures that were in the story. Ask them to predict which sea creatures they could be.
- Ask a child to come up and click on a shell to reveal an animal or creature.
- Ask: *What is this? Is it in the story?*
- If the creature was in the story, ask the children what it did.
- Once all the story creatures and other animals have been revealed, ask the children if they can remember seeing any other sea creatures in the illustrations.
- Look back through the book and see if the children can spot any more.

'Vocabulary focus' activities

Rock-pool rhyming words 👥 👥

- Remind the children that some words in the story rhyme, and give an example (for example, 'sea' and 'me' from the first page).
- Display the interactive activity 'Rock-Pool Rhyming Words'.
- Ask the children to help you to match the rhyming words from the story:
  - Read out the first word.
  - Then go through the second list and ask the children to listen for the rhyming word.
  - Link the two words.
  - Once all the pairs have been linked, read through them with the children and note the matching spelling patterns.

A wonderful home 👥 👥

- Read the repetitive text from page 5 of the story, *One crab.....home for one*.
- Encourage the children to join in with the last line.
- Discuss what 'roaming' means. Use it in other example sentences to help the children's understanding.
- Read the other instances of the repeated phrase (*Romping all over the rock pool...*, *Rollicking all round the rock pool...* and *Rocketing all round the rock pool...*).
- Discuss what 'romping', 'rollicking' and 'rocketing' mean, and again, give examples.
- Ask the children which of these four 'r' words they like most, and why.

EXPLORING THE STORY

'Phonics focus' activity

Shell 'sh' words 👥👥 👥👥

- Before the session, create two matching sets of words cards displaying words containing 'sh' (for example, ship, shell, shop, shed, fish, bash, hush and rush). If possible, create cards in the shape of shells.
- Write out the word 'shell' for the children to see.
- Say the word and then sound it out. Ask the children to copy you.
- Underline the 'sh' and ask the children what sound the two letters make.
- Give each pair of children a word card.
- Ask them to look for the 'sh' in their word before they show their card to the class and point to the 'sh'. Ask which other pair has the matching word.
- Sound out the rest of each word with the class.
- Repeat these steps, until all the word cards have been used.

PHASE 3: Exploring the story through role-play

Session 4: Let's perform a role-play 👥👥 👥👥

During the final session, remind the children of their work so far. Show the story again using the **Storyteller** video on **Connect**, or retell it with the children from the whiteboard. Then ask the children to work together to explore an element of the story in more depth. Focuses for different groups could include:

Crabby movements

- Discuss how crabs normally move, from side to side, scuttling along.
- Encourage the children to try this out across the room.
- Then ask them to use their bodies to explore the ways the hermit crab in the story may move. For example:
  - Scuttling quickly away from the gull
  - With heavy shells on their backs
  - Paddling through the water of the rock pool
- Then put the children into threes, and ask them to link arms, imagining they are held together by one shell. Ask: *What is the best way to walk easily? How can you help one another?*
- Further the session my asking the children to explore ways in which Blob and Brush may move, too.

Rollicking around the rock pool

- Remind the children of what fun the story tells us the crab, Blob and Brush have around the rock pool.
- Mark out an area as a rock pool, perhaps including props as rocks, seaweed or shells.
- Read the repetitive text from page 5 of the story, *One crab.....home for one*.
- Ask the children to pretend to be the crab, and to act out the phrase as you say it. (You may need to remind them what 'roaming' is.)
- Put the children into three groups and allocate each a character (the crab, Blob or Brush).
- Read the other instances of the repeated phrase (*Romping all over the rock pool...*, *Rollicking all round the rock pool...* and *Rocketing all round the rock pool...*).
- Ask the children to make their characters' movements, and to act out the phrase as you say it, interacting with each other.

LITERACY ACTIVITIES

Reading

Beach finds

- Ask mixed-ability pairs to work on the interactive activity 'Beach Finds', selecting the correct words to label the images after an audio prompt.

Differentiation: Encourage less confident readers to listen out for the initial letter of the word and look for it on the word labels.

Word shells

- Copy and cut out shells using Resource Sheet 12.2.
- Create small sets of word cards showing five regular and five tricky words (for example, 'is', 'it', 'in', 'at', 'and', 'no', 'go', 'I', 'the', 'to').
- Give each pair, group or individual a pair of shell shapes and a set of word cards, mixing up the word cards and laying them out.
- Point to a tricky word and a regular word, and discuss why one is tricky to sound out, and the other isn't.
- Ask the children to sort the cards, placing the regular words on one shell and the tricky words on the other shell.
- Discuss how the children sorted their cards, and ways to help them to learn tricky words.

Writing

C is for crab

Hold handwriting sessions based around the initial letters of some of the story's characters:

- Write a large letter 'C' for the children to air-write and then copy, to get the sense of the letter shape.
- Under the letter, write out a sentence for them to copy (for example, 'C is for crab').
- Repeat this, using other animals and settings from the book, focusing on any letters with which children have difficulty.

Sea sentences

- Ask mixed-ability pairs to work on the interactive activity 'Sea Sentences', ordering words to form sentences after audio prompts.
- Once the activity has been completed, ask the children to read out their sentences.

Differentiation: Encourage more confident writers to write their own simple sentences for the characters, composing them orally first.

Phonics Work

Find the missing vowels

- Ask mixed-ability pairs to work on the interactive activity 'Find the Missing Vowels', adding the correct vowels to complete CCVC words with picture prompts.
- Encourage the children to say each word and listen to the vowel sounds, before selecting the correct vowel letter.

Differentiation: More confident children could look at more CCVC and CVCC words and sort them by vowel sounds.

Tentacle 'th' words

- Copy and cut out the anemone word board and letter cards from Resource Sheet 12.3.
- Give a board and set of letter cards to each pair, and ask them to spread the cards out.
- Ask the children to find the two letters that together make the/th/sound.
- Ask them to put the 'th' card on the first tentacle.
- Suggest different words that start with 'th' (for example, 'thin', 'this' and 'them'), asking the children to spell out these words on the tentacles as you say them.
- Sound out the full word with the children, and ask them to write it down.
- Repeat these steps with words that end in 'th' (for example, 'with', 'path' and 'bath').

Differentiation: Encourage more confident children to come up with more 'th' words they can write down. Less confident children can put the words already generated into sentences orally.

CROSS-CURRICULAR ACTIVITIES

Adult-led activities 👥👤

A rock-pool display (Understanding the World; Expressive Arts)

- Create a model rock pool by laying out kitchen foil (as water) surrounded by stones.
- Encourage the children to add artwork to the display by creating any features they admired in the story using craft materials (for example, colourful paper fish, clay shells, card crabs).
- Assist them to add simple labels such as 'crab' and 'sand'.
- Use the display as a place where the children can retell the story.

Shell spirals (Physical Development)

- Explore the spiral pattern of a shell, using your own shell or an image for reference.
- Assist the children to draw spirals (perhaps providing templates to trace, if necessary).
- You could also use chalk to create spiral patterns on the floor outside, for the children to follow.

Paper-plate shells (Expressive Arts)

- Give each child a paper plate that has been cut into a spiral to resemble a snail-type shell.
- Take and print out pictures of the children in crouching poses as they pretend to be hermit crabs.
- Ask the children to decorate their shells using a range of colourful craft materials.
- Once the shells are finished, cut a slot to one side of the plate and add the child's photo to make it appear as though the child is in the shell.

Sea stories (Communication and Language)

- Ask the children to look at specific books in the school library or specific pages online to find more facts or stories about sea creatures.
- Ask groups to discuss them and, if appropriate, to include them in any classroom displays.

Child-led activities 👥👤 👤👤 👤

Salt-dough characters (Expressive Arts)

- Provide modelling dough and encourage the children to make models of the story's three characters.
- Encourage them to think about how each character looks and how they could use the dough to show it (for example, rolled into a sausage for Brush's body or balled to create Blob's body).

Shell sorting (Mathematics)

- Provide a range of different shells and stones for the children to sort as they wish.
- Ask them to explain their categories and series.

Rock-pool tubs (Understanding the World; Communication and Language)

- Create rock pools using water tubs, models of sea creatures, rocks, shells and plants.
- Let the children play freely with the rock pools, perhaps acting out parts of the story.

Sharing a shell (Communication and Language; PSHE)

- Create a large 'shell' that the children are able to hold up (perhaps simply a cardboard box).
- Encourage the children to use it for role-play as the hermit crab and his friends from the story.

SEQUENCE ASSESSMENT

Communication and Language

- Does the child listen to the story with increasing attention and recall?
- Does the child anticipate key events in the story?
- Does the child listen and respond to ideas expressed by others in conversation or discussion?
- Does the child use talk to organise, sequence and clarify thinking and ideas about the story?
- Does the child show evidence of extending their vocabulary?
- Does the child introduce and explore the story in their play?

Reading

- Is the child aware of how the story is structured?
- Can the child describe the main story setting, events and characters?
- Can the child hear and say the initial sounds in words?
- Can the child segment the sounds in simple words and blend them together?

Writing

- Can the child continue a rhyming string?
- Can the child segment the sounds in words and write them down?
- Can the child recognise initial sounds for letters in words?
- Can the child write their own name and simple labels and captions?
- Can the child attempt to write short sentences for a short story?

Review of the Big Picture

At the end of this sequence, discuss with the children what they liked about the story 'Sharing a Shell'. Ask: *Which section or words did you like? Why do you think the creatures wanted to live alone at first? How did the hermit crab, Blob and Brush help each other? What have you learnt from the story?*

Encourage each child to show and explain examples of their writing and reading achievements, and any cross-curricular activities they enjoyed.

Use the 'Pupil observation chart' to record each child's responses and attainment.

SEQUENCE 13 In the Air: Kites

TERM 3 (SUMMER): 1st half term

Main Topic:	In the Air
Subtopic:	Kites
Text Type:	Story-length poem
Main Source Text:	*Blown Away* by Rob Biddulph (ISBN 978-0-007-59382-8)
Approximate Duration:	Two weeks

Big Picture

During this sequence, children will listen to the narrative poem 'Blown Away' and discuss its events, characters, settings, message and rhyming vocabulary as a group.

A range of supportive activities will also give the children an opportunity to explore the poem and its topic in more detail.

Phonics Focuses

The children will practise hearing and saying sounds for words beginning with the/k/sound, and will use their skills in recognising letter sounds to work out the first letters of words. They will also explore simple CCVC words and rhyming patterns, and will develop their blending skills in studying the letter-string 'air'.

Learning Outcomes: See 'Learning Outcomes' Chart, on pages xi–xiv.

Key Vocabulary: maiden flight, brand new, plight, flight, lush, intrepid, crest, companions

Home Links

Encourage children to:
- look at different kites and, with support, try to fly one
- find out more about different kites from around the world
- look at information about the Arctic and the jungle.

Resources Required

Workbook Pages: 27
Resource Sheets 13.1–13.3: Hot or Cold?; k Words; Kite Template

General Resources:
- A kite (or an image of a kite)
- Large images of snowy and jungle scenery
- Sticky tack
- Craft paper
- A box
- Craft materials (e.g. coloured pens, paint, glitter, fabric, tape, glue, string, wool)
- Modelling dough or clay
- Coloured chalk
- Paper streamers
- A tub of water
- Small, simple paper boats of different designs
- Small-world toys (animals, people, boats)

Background Knowledge

Explain to the children that:
- kites can be flown when it is windy, and the wind can pull them very hard. However, it isn't really possible that any of the children could be swept away by a kite!
- flying kites is a hobby in many countries
- In some countries kite flying is very popular, and there are large kite festivals
- the story compares a hot and cold climate and shows through the words and illustrations how each creature is adapted to their different environments. It also looks at how the wind can make things move, such as kites, clouds and sail boats
- penguins are birds that can't fly – but they can swim very well
- penguins, seals and polar bears all live in very cold, snowy places (**NB:** The book shows these animals all living in the same place, which never happens naturally: penguins live in the Antarctic, while polar bears live in the Arctic)
- elephants, giraffes and monkeys all live in warm places with plants to eat.

Performance Ideas and Storytelling Suggestions

- ★ Read through the poem out loud to yourself before reading it to the class, to help you decide where you could add emphasis and intonation to key words or lines (for example, by working out the lines' rhythm and pace and accentuating the exclamations as the kite flies away).
- ★ Use body language and facial expressions to emphasise some of the actions and feelings of the characters.

Sequence Structure

This chart offers suggestions on the order and timings of exploring the story over a two-week period. However, please feel free to adapt the sessions to your own planning and suitable timings for your whole class or set groups.

Exploring the Poem

Tip: If possible, aim to read or show the poem to the children regularly over the two-week period, or before any related activity, so that the children get to know the poem and its messages well.

WEEK 1 (PHASE 1)	WEEKS 1–2 (PHASE 2)	WEEKS 1–2 (PHASE 3)
Introduction to the poem	**Getting to know the poem**	**Exploring the poem through role-play**
All sections could be done in one session or split over two or three sessions.	Aim to hold one or two sessions on getting to know the poem, each retelling the poem and then including your own choice of activities.	Aim to hold one or two sessions at different times across the two-week period.
1. **What do we know?** (approx. 20 minutes) 2. **Let's listen and talk** (approx. 20 minutes) **Extra consolidation activity:** ● Happy homes (approx. 20 minutes)	3. **Let's get to know the poem** (10–15 minutes) **'Structure focus' activities:** ● Sequencing 'Blown Away' (approx. 20 minutes) ● Cold and hot homes ● (20–25 minutes) **'Vocabulary focus' activity:** ● Match the rhymes (approx. 20 minutes) **'Phonics focus' activity:** ● 'k' words (20–25 minutes)	4. **Let's perform a role-play** ● **Kite flying** (approx. 15 minutes) ● **Boat sailing** (approx. 15 minutes) ● **Hot and cold** (approx. 20 minutes)

Literacy Activities

READING	WRITING	PHONICS WORK
● Cloud sentences ● Sorting initial letters	● Writing with 'k' ● What's in the boat?	● Igloo 'air' sounds ● Land and wind

Cross-curricular Activities

Adult-led activities:
- Decorating kites (Expressive Arts)
- Kites around the world (Understanding the World)
- Penguin models (Expressive Arts; Communication and Language)
- Kite games (Communication and Language; Physical Development; PSHE)

Child-led activities:
- Kite hop (Physical Development; Mathematics)
- Blown Away maths (Mathematics)
- Wind investigations (Understanding the World)
- Small-world journeys (Communication and Language)

Sequence Assessment

- Communication and Language
- Reading
- Writing
- Review of the Big Picture

EXPLORING THE POEM

PHASE 1: Introduction to the poem

Session 1: What do we know?

Show the children a kite (or image of a kite). Give prompts and ask open questions to assess the children's current knowledge. For example:

- *What is this?*
- *What kind of weather is best for flying kites?* (Give options, for example, windy/rainy/calm, if children are unsure.)

Discuss the **Background Knowledge** given above. Then explain to the children that they are going to listen to a story-length poem about a penguin called 'Penguin Blue', who is keen to fly his new kite, and do lots of fun activities about kites and the wind.

Session 2: Let's listen and talk

Show the children the kite (or image) again, and remind them briefly of their discussion from the previous session.

Show the **Storyteller** video for 'Blown Away' on **Connect**, or read and perform it to the children (see the **Performance Ideas and Storytelling Suggestions** above).

After the reading, check that the children understand any new or difficult words (see **Key Vocabulary** above). Use some of the new words within sentences relating to things that children recognise to help their understanding.

Ask questions to check the children's understanding of the story. These can be open to group discussion or children can pair with talk partners before reporting back to the group. For example:

- *What pulls Penguin Blue's kite into the sky?*
- *Where is Clive the bear sitting?*

- *Where do they land?*
- *What did Penguin Blue make from the leaves?*
- *Who helps to blow Penguin and his friends home?*
- *Who else is secretly on the boat?*
- *Why do you think Penguin Blue doesn't want to fly another kite?*

Finally, discuss whether or not the children think Penguin Blue and his friends enjoyed their adventure, and if they'd like to find themselves 'blown away' to anywhere specific.

Extra consolidation activity

Happy homes

- Display the final illustration of Penguin Blue and read out the text.
- Ask the children why they think Penguin Blue is happier living in his cold home than in the hot jungle.
- Note the little monkey.
- Ask the children how the monkey is feeling (cold) and how we can tell (it is wearing a hat and scarf, and shivering).
- Ask the children where they think the monkey would rather live.
- Ask talk partners to discuss how the monkey could get back to the jungle, and what she might love to do when she is at home.
- Finally, show the next (and final) image from the book: the monkey flying away home with the kite.

EXPLORING THE POEM

PHASE 2: Getting to know the poem

Session 3: Let's get to know the poem

Show the children the kite (or image) again, and remind them of the poem. Ask them what they remember about it. Retell the poem using the **Storyteller** video on **Connect**, or by reading it aloud to the class. Encourage the children to join in with the 'Whoooosh!' when the elephant blows the sail boat away from the island.

After the retelling, choose focus activities to explore the poem in more depth.

'Structure focus' activities

Sequencing 'Blown Away'

- Display the interactive activity 'Blown Away Story Sequence'.
- Explain that sections of the poem's story have been mixed up and need to be put in the right order.
- Read out each of the four sections and discuss with the children where they are in the poem.
- Drag the sections into order and read through the sequence.
- Ask the children if they are happy with the order, and then (when they are) ask which part of the poem they liked most, and why.

Cold and hot homes

- Cut out the images from Resource Sheet 13.1 and put sticky tack on their backs.
- Display large images of the snowy and jungle scenery.
- Ask the children to suggest words to describe the scenes (for example, 'cold', 'hot', 'white', 'green', 'icy', 'leafy') and write each by the correct image.
- Then show the cut-out images of the animals and ask the children to decide to which setting each belongs, sticking the animals to the scenes as decisions are reached.

'Vocabulary focus' activity

Match the rhymes

- Explain that some of the words in the poem rhyme: they end in the same sounds. Give an example (such as 'me' and 'sea').
- Encourage the children to hear and match other rhyming words from the poem.
- Draw and display two large kite shapes, each divided into four sections.
- Select four pairs of rhyming words, and write one word from each rhyming pair in the sections of the first kite. Write the matching rhymes in the sections of the second kite.
- Focus on the first word in the first kite. Say it, and then ask the children to copy you. Explain that you're going to find its rhyme.
- Read out the four words from the second kite slowly, asking the children to listen and put up their hands when they hear the word that rhymes. Cross off the rhyming words.
- Repeat these steps for each remaining word in the first kite.
- Finally, read through each pair again.

'Phonics focus' activity

'k' words

- Cut out the images from copies of Resource Sheet 13.2, and give a set to each group of children.
- Give each group a a kite shape from Resource Sheet 13.3.
- Ask them to look at each image, and to find the images of things that begin with 'k' (with the/k/sound).
- Once the children have found the correct images, ask them to stick the images into their kite template.
- Ask groups to pair up, showing each other their kites and sounding out the/k/sound for each word.

Differentiation: More confident groups could find words with a 'k' ending and explore the differences in graphemes, for example, ke/ck.

EXPLORING THE POEM

PHASE 3: Exploring the poem through role-play

Session 4: Let's perform a role-play 👥 👥

During the final session, remind the children of their work so far. Show the story again using the **Storyteller** video on **Connect**, or retell it with the children from the whiteboard. Then ask the children to work together to explore an element of the story in more depth. Focuses for different groups could include:

Kite flying

- Suggest that pairs have each been sent a large, invisible box containing their new (invisible) kite.
- Ask the children to open their boxes to get out their new kites.
- Then ask them to mime to your instructions on how to get the kites up in the air, and start making them fly, asking them to imagine that the wind is taking them into air. They have to hold on tight! Ask the children how they feel, while the kites are flying.
- Next, put the children into groups of five.
- Ask one to be the kite flyer, and the others to hold on in a line as they follow an imaginary course around the room.
- Use words to instruct their movements such as 'ducking', 'swaying' and 'floating'.

Boat sailing

- Ask small groups to mime getting into a make-believe boat.
- Make a loud 'Whoooosh!' sound, and ask them to imagine that they are sailing on the sea.
- Describe going over small and then big waves, the boats being tossed and turned, and finally, describe the boats arriving safely at home.

Hot and cold

- Ask the children to imagine how they feel in different temperatures.
- Click your fingers to transport them to a very hot place, and ask them to act out how they feel, encouraging the use of body language and facial expressions (for example, wiping their faces or using their hands to make fanning movements).
- Now click your fingers again to transport the children to a very cold place, again asking them to act out how they feel (for example, shivering or wrapping their arms around themselves).

LITERACY ACTIVITIES

Reading

Cloud sentences

- Ask mixed-ability pairs to work on the interactive activity 'Cloud Sentences' ordering the words to form a sentence after an audio prompt.

Differentiation: Ensure that the children read out the words to check that the sentences make sense before they decide on the final word orders. Encourage less confident readers to look for sounds that they recognise in the words, to help them.

Sorting initial letters

- Cut out the images from Resource Sheet 13.1 (or prepare another set of images of characters and objects from the poem). Place them in a box.
- Prepare or provide a set of letter cards.
- Explain to the children that Penguin Blue has been given a box of pictures and needs to sort them according to their letter sounds.
- Ask the children to take turns removing an image from the box and naming it.
- Ask them to make the initial sound for the image again, and then to pair it under the correct letter.
- Once all the images have been named, go through each letter set, saying the words with the children.

Differentiation: Encourage more confident readers to sound and blend all letters for some of the simpler words.

Writing

Writing with 'k'

- Write a large 'k' on the board, and provide sheets of paper each showing a 'k'.
- Ask the children to air-write the 'k' shape and then to trace over the 'k' shape sheets, before practising writing 'k' on their own.
- Now write out ask the children to complete the sentence, 'k is for _____'.
- Work with the children to sound out and segment the 'k' words they suggest before writing them down.
- Finally, ask groups or pairs to choose one of the words and write out the sentence, drawing a picture to go with it.

Differentiation: Encourage more confident writers to extend the activity by using other letters.

What's in the boat?

- Ask mixed-ability pairs to work on the interactive activity 'What Is in the Boat?', dragging letters into order to spell the name of the animal they see in the boat.

Differentiation: Encourage less confident writers to listen then say the name of the animal and isolate the initial-letter sound first.

Phonics Work

Igloo 'air' sounds

- Ask mixed-ability pairs to work on the interactive activity 'Igloo Sounds', identifying the words containing the letter-string 'air'.
- Once the children have completed the task, ask them to read out each 'air' word to you and to use them in oral sentences.

Land and wind

- Write out the words 'land' and 'wind' for the children to see, and underline the 'nd' ending.
- Ask children if they can think of any other words that end 'nd' (for example, 'band', 'hand', 'sand', ' 'bend', 'lend' and 'send').
- If prompts are needed, write out sample words omitting the vowels, and ask the children to complete them by choosing what vowel would create a word.
- Prepare or provide a set of letter cards.
- Ask groups to form the 'nd' words using the cards, and then to try writing them out.

Differentiation: Ask more confident children to move on to words ending in 'sh'. Ask less confident children to focus on CVC words as appropriate.

CROSS-CURRICULAR ACTIVITIES

Adult-led activities 👥👤

Decorating kites (Expressive Arts)

- Provide large paper kite shapes, and ask the children to decorate their own kites, to making them as eye-catching and colourful as possible.
- Examples could include using chalks on black paper and smudging the colours in with fingers; blow painting; finger or hand printing designs; swirly, stripy patterns; funny faces; collage materials; glitter kites, and so on.
- Hang the kites around the room with colourful strings.

Kites around the world (Understanding the World)

- Search online to find a video of kite festivals around the world (for example, the international kite festival in Gujarat, India).
- Watch the video with the children and discuss all the different types, colours and sizes of the kites.

Penguin models (Expressive Arts; Communication and Language)

- Ask the children to make models of Penguin Blue, his friends and his igloo using modelling dough or clay.
- Give out balls of black and white modelling clay. Show the children how to form a penguin body and a head using just the black clay and then add on flat pieces of white clay for eyes and front of body. Add a beak in orange or yellow.
- Put groups together and ask them to form a snowy home scene with their models.

Kite games (Communication and Language; Physical Development; PSHE)

- If appropriate weather occurs, allow the children the opportunity to fly a kite, or to watch one being flown.
- Alternatively, play 'musical kites', asking the children to pretend to be kites while the music is on, and to fall to ground when the music stops.

Child-led activities 👥👤 👤👤 👤

Kite hop (Physical Development; Mathematics)

- Outside, draw large kite shapes on the ground with different colours of chalk.
- Ask the children to hop from one to another, without touching the ground in between.
- Suggest that they then draw their own kite shapes in whatever patterns they want.
- Watch how they play. What sequences do they use?

Blown Away maths (Mathematics)

- Draw and display some kite shapes, and colour them in in a pattern.
- Ask the children to continue the colour pattern using copies of Resource Sheet 13.3.
- Have kite/clouds themed maths sessions, for example, an odd one out kite shape in a line of kite shapes; match the shape or colour of kites; cloud shapes for addition and subtraction activities.

Wind investigations (Understanding the World)

- Hold up streamers in the wind (or by a fan) and ask the children to comment on how they move.
- Set up a tub of water with small paper boats, and ask the children to experiment with how blowing the boats can move them. What shapes of boat move fastest?

Small-world journeys (Communication and Language)

- Ask the children to retell 'Blown Away' in their own words using small-world toys (including different animals and/or human characters).
- Encourage them to use classroom objects and/or craft materials to create the different settings. Lay out white cloth for the ice, blue for the sea and green for the jungle.

SEQUENCE ASSESSMENT

Communication and Language
- Does the child use language to imagine and recreate roles and experiences in play situations?
- Does the child introduce and explore the poem's storyline in their play?
- Does the child listen and respond to ideas expressed by others in conversation or discussion?
- Does the child use talk to organise, sequence and clarify thinking and ideas about the poem?

Reading
- Can the child describe the main setting, events and characters of the poem?
- Can the child hear and say the initial sounds in words?
- Can the child segment the sounds in simple words and blend them together?
- Can the child begin to read words and simple sentences?

Writing
- Can the child blend sounds for words and write them down?
- Can the child recognise initial sounds for letters in words?
- Can the child write their own name and simple labels and captions?
- Can the child attempt to write short sentences for a short story?

Review of the Big Picture
At the end of this sequence, discuss with the children what happened in 'Blown Away', in the correct sequence. Ask: *Where did Penguin Blue live? To where did he travel? Why did he prefer to stay at home? What did you like most about the poem?*

Encourage each child to show and explain examples of their writing and reading achievements, and any cross-curricular activities they enjoyed.

Use the 'Pupil observation chart' to record each child's responses and attainment.

SEQUENCE 14 In the Air: Magical Flying!

TERM 3 (SUMMER): 1st half term

Main Topic:	In the Air
Subtopic:	Magical Flying!
Text Type:	Story
Main Source Text:	*The Magic Bed* by John Burningham (ISBN 978-0-099-43969-1)
Extra Source Text:	*The Crocodile Under the Bed* by Judith Kerr (ISBN 978-0-007-58675-2)
Approximate Duration:	Two weeks

Big Picture

During this sequence, children will listen to the story 'The Magic Bed' and discuss its events, characters, settings, message and vocabulary as a group.

A range of supportive activities will also give the children an opportunity to explore the story, and their own imaginations, in more detail.

Phonics Focuses

The children will practise hearing and saying sounds for words that begin with the/m/sound, and will use their skills in recognising letter sounds to work out the first letters of words. They will also explore simple CCVC words (such as 'skip', 'swim' and 'shop'), and explore CVC letter patterns.

Learning Outcomes: See 'Learning Outcomes' Chart, on pages xi–xiv.

Key Vocabulary: magic, furniture, Amazon, gnome, dolphin, dump, skip

Home Links

Encourage children to:

- look at and describe their own beds
- discuss where they would go on a magic bed
- listen to, read or look at other stories about magical flying.

Resources Required

Workbook Pages: 6–8, 15–18

Resource Sheets 14.1–14.3: Sequencing 'The Magic Bed'; Magic Objects; My Magic Object

General Resources:

- A pillow
- Craft paper
- String
- Pegs
- Craft materials (e.g. coloured pens and pencils, fabric, patterned/coloured paper, newspaper, tape, glue, paint, empty matchboxes, cardboard)
- Counters
- Small-world toys (e.g. animals and people)

Background Knowledge

Explain to the children that:

- 'The Magic Bed' is a fantasy story: beds cannot really travel by magic. However, there is a kind of magical travelling we all do in bed when we're asleep, when we dream
- dreaming is thought to be the mind's way of processing some of the thoughts we have and the complicated information we take in, often in the form of strange and mysterious stories.

Performance Ideas and Storytelling Suggestions

★ Read through the story out loud to yourself before reading it to the class, to help you decide where you could add emphasis and intonation to key words or lines (for example, by saying the 'm' words as if Georgie is trying hard to find the right one, or by using different voices for each type of animal).

★ Use body language and facial expressions to emphasise some of the actions and feelings of the characters.

Sequence Structure

This chart offers suggestions on the order and timings of exploring the story over a two-week period. However, please feel free to adapt the sessions to your own planning and suitable timings for your whole class or set groups.

Exploring the Story

Tip: If possible, aim to read or show the story to the children regularly over the two-week period, or before any related activity, so that the children get to know the story and its messages well.

WEEK 1 (PHASE 1)	WEEKS 1–2 (PHASE 2)	WEEKS 1–2 (PHASE 3)
Introduction to the story	**Getting to know the story**	**Exploring the story through role-play**
All sections could be done in one session or split over two or three sessions.	Aim to hold one or two sessions on getting to know the story, each retelling the story and then including your own choice of activities.	Aim to hold one or two sessions at different times across the two-week period.
1. **What do we know?** (approx. 20 minutes) 2. **Let's listen and talk** (approx. 20 minutes) **Extra consolidation activity:** ● What happened next? (approx. 30 minutes)	3. **Let's get to know the story** (10–15 minutes) **'Structure focus' activity:** ● Sequencing 'The Magic Bed' (approx. 30 minutes) **'Vocabulary focus' activities:** ● 'The Magic Bed' characters and places (approx. 15 minutes) ● My magic 'm' word (approx. 20 minutes) **'Phonics focus' activity:** ● 'm' words (approx. 15 minutes)	4. **Let's perform a role-play** ● **A magic journey** (30–40 minutes) ● **The lost tiger** (30–45 minutes)

Literacy Activities

READING	WRITING	PHONICS WORK
● What's in the shop? ● Journey sentences	● My magic object ● I can see…	● Odd words out ● Making new words

Cross-curricular Activities

Adult-led activities:	Child-led activities:
● Imaginary journeys (Expressive Arts) ● Thank-you cards (Expressive Arts) ● Places from above (Understanding the World) ● Who's on the bed? (Mathematics)	● Our magic bed (Communication and Language) ● Bed models (Expressive Arts) ● Small-world magical flying (Communication and Language; PSHE; Expressive Arts)

Sequence Assessment

● Communication and Language
● Reading
● Writing
● Review of the Big Picture

EXPLORING THE STORY

PHASE 1: Introduction to the story

Session 1: What do we know?

Show the children the pillow and a bed cover. Give prompts and ask open questions to assess the children's current knowledge. For example:

- *What is this?*
- *Where would you usually find a pillow?*
- *What does your bed look like?*
- *What do you like most about your bed?*
- *Where did your bed come from, and how long have you had it?*

Discuss the **Background Knowledge** given above, and ask the children to discuss their most memorable dreams.

Then explain to the children that they are going to listen to a story about a boy who is going to get his first big bed and do lots of fun activities connected with it. Emphasise that this boy's bed is very special because it is magical, and encourage the children to predict how it could be magical.

Session 2: Let's listen and talk

Show the children the pillow again, and remind them briefly of their discussion from the previous session.

Show the **Storyteller** video for 'The Magic Bed' on **Connect**, or read the story yourself (see the **Performance Ideas and Storytelling Suggestions** above).

After the reading, check that the children understand any new or difficult words (see **Key Vocabulary** above).

Ask questions to check the children's understanding of the story. These can be open to group discussion or children can pair with talk partners before reporting back to the group. For example:

- *Where does Georgie get his bed?*
- *What can the bed do?*
- *Why is the little tiger sad?*

- *What does Georgie find in the cave?*
- *What birds get a lift on his bed?*
- *Where has Granny sent Georgie's magic bed?*
- *How do you think Georgie felt when he got his magic bed back?*

Finally, discuss places the children would most like to see if they had magic beds of their own.

Extra consolidation activity

What happened next?

- Remind the children that Georgie is about to have another magic bed journey at the end of the story.
- Ask them to think about where the bed might be going. Ask: *What will Georgie do, and who could he meet?*
- Ask the children (either with you, as a whole class, or in groups) to come up with a new journey adventure. Ensure they are encouraged to develop their ideas.
- If the children are working in groups, ask them to feed their ideas back to the class.
- If time allows, ask them to draw pictures of the journey, which could be displayed with captions.

EXPLORING THE STORY

PHASE 2: Getting to know the story

Session 3: Let's get to know the story 👥 👥

Show the children the pillow again, and remind them of the story. Ask them what they remember about it. Retell the story using the **Storyteller** video on **Connect**, or read the story yourself.

After the retelling, spend some time asking questions and discussing Georgie's character. For example:

- *How do you think Georgie felt about getting a new bed?*
- *How do you think he felt when the bed first started to fly?*
- *Do you think Georgie was a kind person? What tells us this?*
- *How do you think Georgie felt when his bed was sent to the dump?*
- *Which journey do you think he liked most, and why?*

Then choose focus activities to explore the story in more depth.

'Structure focus' activity

Sequencing 'The Magic Bed' 👥 👥

- Cut out the cards from Resource Sheet 14.1 and place them around the room in the correct story sequence. Mark out a clear path for the children to walk.
- Ask the children to join you on a 'magic bed' journey, to help you to retell the story.
- Say: *In this bed you will travel far. First say your prayers and then say…*, and add an m–y word of your choice (for example, 'money', 'matey', 'mummy').
- Ask the children to follow you to the first card.
- At the first card, ask the children what it shows (the shop) and encourage them to tell you the first part of the story, during which Georgie gets the bed.
- Say the rhyme again and move on with the journey to the next card. Again, ask the children what it shows and ask them to explain to you what happened next in the story.
- Repeat these steps until all cards have been collected and the story has been completely retold.
- Display the cards in sequence order.

'Vocabulary focus' activities

'Magic Bed' characters and places 👥 👥

- Display the interactive activity 'Magic Bed Characters and Places'.
- Read out the list of some characters that appear in the story.
- Explain that they are lost and need to get back to their places.
- Ask the children to match the characters to their correct places.

My magic 'm' word 👥 👥

- Remind the children that Georgie had to use a magic 'm' word to get the bed to fly.
- Ask talk partners to come up with their own magic 'm' words. (They could end with 'Y' too.)
- Ask pairs to feed back to the class as you write out all the magic words.
- Hang their magic words under a cut out of a bed or an 'M' and hang it up as a mobile, or place them around an image of a bed on a display board.

Differentiation: Ask more confident writers to write out (and decorate) their magic words.

'Phonics focus' activity

'm' words 👥 👥

- Display the interactive activity 'M Words'.
- Look at the images and listen to the 'm' words next to them.
- Ask the children to decide which is the matching word for each image, and click to reveal the word.
- After the activity is complete, ask the children to help you to sound out and blend the letters for the words 'mist', 'mill' and 'moss'.
- Write out the words as they are being blended. More confident writers could write out the words on mini whiteboards.

EXPLORING THE STORY

PHASE 3: Exploring the story through role-play

Session 4: Let's perform a role-play 👥 👥

During the final session, remind the children of their work so far. Show the story again, using the **Storyteller** video on **Connect**, or retell it with the children from the whiteboard. Then ask the children to work together to explore an element of the story in more depth. Focuses for different groups could include:

A magic journey

- Tell the story of a new magic journey for the children to mime out. It could be a journey that has been discussed in the **Extra consolidation activity** for Phase 1 (if completed) or one developed for the session (for example, a journey to meet fairy-tale characters or to Australia to help a kangaroo).
- Talk about the journey, and suggest actions for the children to make (for example, as waving at passing birds or shivering as they fly through a rain cloud).
- Ask various children how they feel, and others what could happen next.
- Finish the session by describing flying home, with new sights and experiences along the way.

The lost tiger

- Focus on Georgie's journey to help the lost tiger.
- Put the children into pairs, asking one to play Georgie and the other to play the young tiger.
- Ask them to act out the scene in which the young tiger is upset and is lost, giving prompts as needed (for example, *Why did the tiger wander away from home? What does Georgie say and do to make the tiger feel better?*)
- Finally, describe and ask the children to mime the flight back to the tiger's house.

LITERACY ACTIVITIES

Reading

What's in the shop?

- Ask mixed-ability pairs to work on the interactive activity 'What's in the Shop?', matching labels to objects after an audio prompt.

Differentiation: Ask more confident readers to take a lead in sounding out and blending the words for the labels that were already in place on the shelves, and encourage others to join in.

Journey sentences

- Create separate word cards that, when put together, make up a simple sentence (such as 'The bed is in the shop.' or 'The bed will land on the hill.').
- Place the word cards around the room.
- Ask the children to find the cards, letting them know how many cards there are to find.
- Once all the cards have been collected, ask the finders to read each one out.
- Guide them as they work together to sort them into the sentence.

Differentiation: Ask all children to note the full stop and capital letter. Have more confident children peer-support reading in pairs taking a lead and encouraging participation. Before less confident readers try to form the sentence from the cards, say it for them.

Writing

My magic object

- Cut out the images from Resource Sheet 14.2 and lay them out in front of the children.
- Look at each object and ask the children what it is.
- Ask the children to help you write a label for each one, encouraging them to sound out and segment the letters as you (or they) write.
- Ask which object the children would like to be magic, and to take them on journeys. Discuss why.
- Hand out copies of Resource Sheet 14.3 and ask the children to complete the sentence by writing in the name of their magic object and drawing it in the blank space.

I can see...

- Ask mixed-ability pairs to work on the interactive activity 'I Can See...', ordering the letters to complete the labels of the images they may see from the magic bed.

Differentiation: Encourage less confident writers to sound out the initial letters of the words first, to help them work out the letter order.

Phonics Work

Odd words out

- Ask mixed-ability pairs to work on the interactive activity 'Words with 'ch'', identifying the words that contain the grapheme 'ch'.

Differentiation: More confident children could explore and write down as many other 'ch' words as they can, in pairs or groups.

Making new words

- Prepare or provide a set of letter cards that could make words with the VC -ed pattern.
- Ask the children to use them to make the word 'bed', encouraging them to sound out and blend the letters as they put them out.
- Take away the 'b' and ask the children to find other letters they could add in its place, to make new words (for example, 'fed', 'led' or 'red').

Differentiation: Encourage more confident children to explore what words they could make by substituting letters for the 'd' or 'e' instead.

CROSS-CURRICULAR ACTIV1ITIES

Adult-led activities 👥👥 👥 👤

Imaginary journeys (Expressive Arts)

- Ask talk partners to imagine their own journeys on the magic bed.
- Discuss their ideas as a class, giving suggestions if necessary (for example, under the sea, seeing dinosaurs or visiting family members who live far away).
- Then ask the children to paint or draw their own imaginary journeys, encouraging them to describe the setting as they do so.

Thank-you cards (Expressive Arts)

- Remind the children of the ways in which Georgie helped other characters in the story.
- Ask them to make and decorate thank-you cards or an invitation to come over to tea from the gnomes, fairies, tiger or geese.
- Model a sentence for them to write or adapt (for example, 'Thank you, Georgie!', 'Come to tea.') and encourage them to write their names in the cards.

Places from above (Understanding the World)

- Ask the children to think about what Georgie could see when he was flying high up.
- Use the computer to show locations from above, for example, using an online maps service.
- Start with a local area with which the children are familiar and then move on to other settings.
- Ask the children what they can see, and how they think things look different from above.

Who's on the bed? (Mathematics)

- Draw out a large image of a bed with a quilt as a counting board (this may simply be a partitioned rectangle).
- Ask groups to put different numbers of counters or small-world toys on the bed and/or its different sections.
- Use this to create simple whole-class addition and subtraction tasks.
- Finally, ask the children to estimate the number of counters or toys that will fit on the bed and/or its different sections.

Child-led activities 👥👥 👥 👤

Our magic bed (Communication and Language)

- Set up a makeshift bed for the children to sit on and play with. (If this is impractical, simply lay out a blanket.)
- Encourage them to act out the story or to imagine their own magical journeys.
- Lay out a decorated rug and suggest that this could be a magic carpet that goes on a magic journey.

Bed models (Expressive Arts)

- Supply craft materials, and ask the children to make models of magic beds.
- Encourage them to add bedding, using cloth or coloured paper, and decorate them further.
- These could then be used during small-world play (see below).
- You may also want to hang all the model beds around the ceiling.

Small-world magical flying (Communication and Language; PSHE; Expressive Arts)

- Put out small play characters and objects for the children to use for their own imaginary journey places and magical experiences.
- Watch how they play. Do they use the language and story ideas in their own journeys or are they retelling the story?

SEQUENCE ASSESSMENT

Communication and Language

- Does the child use language to imagine and recreate roles and experiences in play situations?
- Does the child introduce and explore the story in their play?
- Does the child listen and respond to ideas expressed by others in conversation or discussion?
- Does the child use talk to organise, sequence and clarify thinking and ideas about the story?

Reading

- Can the child describe the main settings, events and characters of the story?
- Can the child hear and say the initial sounds in words?
- Can the child segment the sounds in simple words and blend them together?
- Can the child begin to read words and simple sentences?

Writing

- Can the child blend sounds for words and write them down?
- Can the child recognise initial sounds for letters in words?
- Can the child write their own name and simple labels and captions?
- Can the child attempt to write short sentences for a short story?

Review of the Big Picture

At the end of this sequence, discuss with the children what they liked about 'The Magic Bed'. Ask: *Where did Georgie go and who did he meet? Which magic trip did you like most? What do you think of Georgie? What magical journeys did you like imagining?*

Encourage each child to show and explain examples of their writing and reading achievements, and any cross-curricular activities they enjoyed.

Use the 'Pupil observation chart' to record each child's responses and attainment.

SEQUENCE 15 In the Air: Space and Stars

TERM 3 (SUMMER): 1st half term

Main Topic:	In the Air
Subtopic:	Space and Stars
Text Type:	Story
Main Source Text:	*How to Catch a Star* by Oliver Jeffers (ISBN 978-0-007-15034-2)
Extra Source Text:	*Whatever Next!* by Jill Murphy (ISBN 978-0-230-01547-0)
Approximate Duration:	Two weeks

Big Picture

During this sequence, children will listen to the story 'How to Catch a Star' and discuss its messages, main character and sequence of events as a group.

A range of supportive activities will also give the children an opportunity to explore the story in more detail, and to find out more about stars and space.

Phonics Focuses

The children will practise recognising letter sounds to work out words' first letters, and will investigate simple rhyming spelling patterns. They will also begin to recognise and decode words that contain the phonemes /ar/, /igh/ and long /oo/.

Learning Outcomes: See 'Learning Outcomes' Chart, on pages xi–xiv.

Key Vocabulary: star, life belt, spaceship, petrol, seagull, prettiest, jetty

Home Links

Encourage children to:

- look up in the night sky to observe the stars and see patterns in them
- find out more about stars and the moon
- look at and listen to other stories about space and the stars.

Resources Required

Workbook Pages: 20–22, 29–30

Resource Sheets 15.1–15.2: The Boy's Day; Space Labels

General Resources:

- A large, shiny star shape – e.g. cut from cardboard and covered in kitchen foil
- Craft paper (coloured, including black)
- Thick card
- Craft materials (e.g. paint, glitter, fabric, coloured pens and pencils, coloured chalk, patterned/coloured paper, newspaper, tape, glue)
- A bag
- A pin
- Torches
- Star-shaped and round biscuit cutters
- Air-drying clay
- A hole-punch
- Wool or string
- Small-world toys (e.g. people, boats, rockets, trees)

Background Knowledge

Explain to the children that:

- stars look small and twinkly to us, but they are really whole suns that are burning with fire, millions of miles away from Earth. We could never pick up a star!
- it looks like we can see a lot of stars from Earth, but this is only a tiny number of all the stars in space – even only in Earth's galaxy, the Milky Way
- there are billions of stars in a galaxy, and billions of galaxies in the universe!
- this story, about a boy's wish to catch a star so it can be his friend, is perfect for discussion on patience, expectations and exploring stars and other things in the night sky.

Performance Ideas and Storytelling Suggestions

- ★ Read through the story out loud to yourself before reading it to the class, to help you decide where you could add emphasis and intonation to key words or lines.

- ★ Read each page slowly, adding emphasis to phrases that include ellipses (three dots) to draw attention to how long the boy is waiting.
- ★ Use your voice to convey the different moods of the boy, from frustration to happiness.

Sequence Structure

This chart offers suggestions on the order and timings of exploring the story over a two-week period. However, please feel free to adapt the sessions to your own planning and suitable timings for your whole class or set groups.

Exploring the Story

Tip: If possible, aim to read or show the story to the children regularly over the two-week period, or before any related activity, so that the children get to know the story and its messages well.

WEEK 1 (PHASE 1)	WEEKS 1–2 (PHASE 2)	WEEKS 1–2 (PHASE 3)
Introduction to the story	**Getting to know the story**	**Exploring the story through role-play**
All sections could be done in one session or split over two or three sessions.	Aim to hold one or two sessions on getting to know the story, each retelling the story and then including your own choice of activities.	Aim to hold one or two sessions at different times across the two-week period.
1. **What do we know?** (approx. 15 minutes) 2. **Let's listen and talk** (approx. 20 minutes) **Extra consolidation activity:** ● Catching a star (20–25 minutes)	3. **Let's get to know the story** (10–15 minutes) **'Structure focus' activities:** ● Sequencing the boy's day (20–25 minutes) ● The boy's moods (approx. 15 minutes) **'Vocabulary focus' activity:** ● Space labels (20–25 minutes) **'Phonics focus' activity:** ● Catching 'ar' words (approx. 20 minutes)	4. **Let's perform a role-play** ● **Mood mime** (30–40 minutes) ● **How to catch a star** (30–40 minutes) ● **Rocket adventure** (30–40 minutes)

Literacy Activities

READING	WRITING	PHONICS WORK
● Space sentences ● Star words	● Where is the star? ● Naming stars	● Mixed-up rockets ● Catching 'igh' words

Cross-curricular Activities

Adult-led activities:	Child-led activities:
● Star rhymes (Expressive Arts) ● Star lights (Understanding the World) ● Find the star (Communication and Language; Physical Development) ● Exploring space (Understanding the World)	● Making stars (Expressive Arts) ● Star shapes (Mathematics) ● Small-world star-catching (PSHE; Expressive Arts; Communication and Language)

Sequence Assessment

● Communication and Language
● Reading
● Writing
● Review of the Big Picture

EXPLORING THE STORY

PHASE 1: Introduction to the story

Session 1: What do we know?

Show the children the large, shiny star shape. Give prompts and ask open questions to assess the children's current knowledge about stars and space. For example:

- *What is this?*
- *Where might you see stars?*
- *What time of day can we see stars?*
- *Have you ever watched the stars? What do they look like?*

Discuss the **Background Knowledge** given above, and discuss what other things might be seen at night, such as the moon and planets.

Then explain to the children that they are going to listen to a story about a boy who loved watching stars so much that he wanted to catch one. Ask the children: *How do you think he could catch a star?*

Session 2: Let's listen and talk

Show the children the star again, and remind them briefly of their discussion from the previous session.

Show the **Storyteller** video for 'How to Catch a Star' on **Connect**, or read the story yourself (see the **Performance Ideas and Storytelling Suggestions** above).

After the reading, check that the children understand any new or difficult words (see **Key Vocabulary** above).

Ask questions to check the children's understanding of the story. These can be open to group discussion or children can pair with talk partners before reporting back to the group. For example:

- *From where did the boy watch the stars?*
- *What did he want to do with a star of his own?*
- *What did the boy try to climb, to get the star?*

- *Why couldn't he use his spaceship?*
- *How did the boy try and get the star out of the water? What was this star?* (a reflection)
- *Where did he find a star in the end? What was this star?* (a starfish)
- *How was the boy feeling at the end of the story? Why?*

Finally, ask the children to discuss whether they would like a star of their own, and what they would like to do with it.

Extra consolidation activity

Catching a star

- Ask the children to imagine they are catching a star. Ask them to join in as you hold up your hands in the air and pretend to catch a star. Model looking at it with wonder and with care, as if it is very precious.
- Ask the children how their star looks (for example, bright, shiny, yellowy, glittery).
- Now model touching the star gently.
- Ask the children how their star feels.
- Ask talk partners to discuss what games they could play with their new stars, before feeding back to the class.

EXPLORING THE STORY

PHASE 2: Getting to know the story

Session 3: Let's get to know the story 👥 👥

Show the children the pillow again, and remind them of the story. Ask them what they remember about it. Retell the story using the **Storyteller** video on **Connect**, or read the story yourself.

After the retelling, choose focus activities to explore the story in more depth.

'Structure focus' activities

Sequencing the boy's day 👥 👥

- Create a long strip of coloured paper, or paper coloured with pencils or chalk, that represents the changing sky during the story (dark for the night sky, yellowish-blue for the sunrise, blue for most of the day, orange for the sunset and purple for the early night sky).
- Cut out the images from Resource Sheet 15.1.
- Work with the children to re-create the timeline of the story on the sky strip, using the images.
- Discuss what happened at each point. Ask: *Why could the boy see the star only when it was darker?* (The sun is brighter than the stars, so its light overpowers theirs.)

The boy's moods 👥 👥

- Display the interactive activity 'The Boy's Moods'.
- Remind the children that the boy's mood changed during the story.
- Ask the children to listen to events from the story that affected the boy's mood.
- Ask them to select the happy face or sad face by each sentence, to show how his mood was affected.
- At the end of the activity, retell the story briefly and ask why the boy was happy at the end.

'Vocabulary focus' activity

Space labels 👥 👥

- Ask the children to help you create a space scene using the images from Resource Sheet 15.2.
- Lay out the images and word cards on black craft paper.
- Hold up an image, such as a rocket, and ask the children what it could be. (**NB:** The story uses the word 'spaceship' but the label uses 'rocket' as this is easier to decode.)
- Add it to the background.
- Once all the images are on the board, look at the labels. Point to the rocket. Encourage the children to look for a label beginning with 'r' and then sound and blend out the words with them. Add the label to the image.
- Once the activity is complete, discuss which space words were used in the story, and where.

'Phonics focus' activity

Catching 'ar' words 👥 👥

- Display the interactive activity 'Catching 'ar' Words'.
- Note the large star in the middle, containing the word 'star'.
- Sound out the word, using a finger to point to the graphemes as you say the phonemes.
- Ask the children to say the /ar/ sound.
- Look at the other stars and the words inside them, working with the children to sound out the words.
- Ask the children to help you to select the ones that contain the /ar/ sound.

Differentiation: If your class requires support with 'ar' words, ask them to create a class word mobile displaying these words in stars, as reminders.

EXPLORING THE STORY

PHASE 3: Exploring the story through role-play

Session 4: Let's perform a role-play

During the final session, remind the children of their work so far. Show the story again using the **Storyteller** video on **Connect**, or retell it with the children from the whiteboard. Then ask the children to work together to explore an element of the story in more depth. Focuses for different groups could include:

Mood mime

- Read out the story for the children to follow.
- Ask them to focus on how the boy feels at each point, and to mime his mood.
- How would they show the boy being sad and then happy?

How to catch a star

- Ask the children to pretend that they are trying to catch a star. How would they do it?
- Encourage them to mime jumping up, climbing trees, throwing a hoop, zooming up to space and trying to persuade a bird to help, just as the boy in the story did.
- Then ask them to experiment with other methods – what other ideas could they try?

Rocket adventure

- Ask small groups to form rocket shapes (for example, a group of five could form as two pairs with a single child at the front).
- Count down to take-off, asking the children to join in.
- Ask them to mime taking off into space.
- Once the rockets are flying, suggest different situations they could encounter (such as comets zooming past, or landing on the moon).
- Ask various children how they feel, and others what could happen next.
- Finish the session by describing flying home, with new sights and experiences along the way.

LITERACY ACTIVITIES

Reading

Space sentences

- Ask mixed-ability pairs to work on the interactive activity 'Space Sentences', dragging the missing words to complete the sentences.

Differentiation: Encourage less confident readers to sound out the initial letters as well as predicting the missing words, to help with reading skills.

Star words

- Create 12 star-shaped cards and write six pairs of rhyming word patterns into them (for example, 'rocket'/'pocket'; 'sun'/'bun'; 'star'/'car'; 'moon'/'spoon'; 'hand'/'sand' and 'high'/'sigh').
- Ask the children to sound out the words, with or without support, and point to the rhyming letter patterns.
- Then shuffle the cards and lay them out, asking the children to find the matching pairs.
- Alternatively, use the cards to play a game of rhyming 'Snap!'.
- Put large star word cards on the floor for the children to jump onto rhyming pairs, or hang them up for the children to reach up and grab.

Writing

Where is the star?

- Ask mixed-ability pairs to work on the interactive activity 'Where is the Star?', dragging graphemes into order to create a word after a visual prompt.

Differentiation: Encourage more confident children to make up their own oral sentences describing where else the star could be. More confident writers could sound out and segment simple words and write their sentences.

Naming stars

- Explain to the children that you are giving them each a star to keep.
- Give each child a star cut from thick card, to colour in and decorate.
- Once they have completed their stars, ask the children to write, once modelled: 'This star belongs to _____.'
- Ask them to complete their sentences with their names, and to attach them to their stars for display.

Differentiation: Provide key words to support independent sentence making for less confident writers.

Phonics Work

Mixed-up rockets

- Ask mixed-ability pairs to work on the interactive activity 'Mixed-Up Rockets', sorting the words according to whether they contain 'oo' or 'ar' after an audio prompt.
- Ask the children to sound out and read each word once they have completed the activity.

Differentiation: Encourage less confident children blend the initial letters and the 'ar' or 'oo' letter patterns to help them to work out the words.

Catching 'igh' words

- Make star-shaped letter cards for the letters 'n', 'l', 'm', 's', 'r' and 't'.
- Make six more cards that all say 'ight'.
- Place the 'ight' cards in a vertical line on a table.
- Sound out and blend the 'ight' letter string with the children.
- Place the single letters into a bag.
- Ask the children to take turns to pull out a letter and place it in front of one of the 'ight' cards.
- Ask the children to sound out and blend the letters to say each word made.

Differentiation: More confident children may suggest other 'igh' words (such as 'high', 'sigh', 'flight').

CROSS-CURRICULAR ACTIVITIES

Adult-led activities 👥

Star rhymes (Expressive Arts)

- Introduce nursery rhymes or songs about stars and the moon (for example, 'Twinkle, Twinkle, Little Star', 'When You Wish Upon a Star', 'Hey Diddle, Diddle').
- Use instruments to create clear beats.
- As a class, find actions to go with the words.

Star lights (Understanding the World)

- Make holes in thick paper to represent stars. (You could do this in the shape of real constellations.)
- Shine torches through the holes, to see the light and reflections on another surface, for example, water or a wall.
- Explore what surfaces reflect the lights the best.

Find the star (Communication and Language; Physical Development)

- Hide the large, shiny star in the classroom or outside.
- Guide groups to find it using 'hot' and 'cold' clues.
- Then encourage children to hide stars for each other, and to guide each other in a similar way.

Exploring space (Understanding the World)

- Ask the children to look at specific books in the school library or specific pages online to find more facts or stories about space.
- Ask groups to discuss them.
- Display what they have found in a designated classroom area.

Child-led activities 👥 👥 👤

Making stars (Expressive Arts)

- Ask the children to use use star-shaped biscuit cutters to cut out air-drying clay into stars, and round cutters to make moon shapes.
- Let them decorate their stars using craft materials such as coloured paints and glitter.
- Hang the stars around the room.

Star shapes (Mathematics)

- Use a hole-punch to punch out a star design on card.
- Ask the children to lace wool or string through the holes to make the shape.
- Further develop skills in drawing shapes by asking them to draw around different star shapes. How many stars can they make? How many points are there on each star?

Small-world star-catching (PSHE; Communication and Language; Expressive Arts)

- Ask the children to use small-world toys to play out the story, supplying craft materials to assist them (for example, blue cloth to be used as water).
- They may wish to make extra props to use, such as a rocket.
- Then encourage the children to create their own stories about someone who wants something impossible (such as the sun or moon).

SEQUENCE ASSESSMENT

Communication and Language

- Does the child use language to imagine and recreate roles and experiences in play situations?
- Does the child introduce and explore the story in their play?
- Does the child listen and respond to ideas expressed by others in conversation or discussion?
- Does the child use talk to organise, sequence and clarify thinking and ideas about the story?

Reading

- Can the child describe the main settings, events and characters of the story?
- Can the child hear and say the initial sounds in words?
- Can the child segment the sounds in simple words and blend them together?
- Can the child begin to read words and simple sentences?
- Does the child know that information can also be retrieved from books and computers?

Writing

- Can the child segment and blend sounds for words and write them down?
- Can the child recognise initial sounds for letters in words?
- Can the child write their own name and simple labels and captions?
- Can the child attempt to write short sentences?

Review of the Big Picture

At the end of this sequence, discuss with the children what happened in the story and in what order. Ask: *How did the boy try to catch a star? What time of day was it when he saw one? What were the boy's feelings at the beginning, middle and end of the story?*

Encourage each child to show and explain examples of their writing and reading achievements, and any cross-curricular activities they enjoyed.

Use the 'Pupil observation chart' to record each child's responses and attainment.

SEQUENCE 16 Our World: Fairs and Carnivals

TERM 3 (SUMMER) 2nd half term

Main Topic:	Our World
Subtopic:	Fairs and Carnivals
Text Type:	Poem
Main Source Text:	'The Big Steel Band' by Wes Magee, from *The Chinese Dragon and Other Poems about Festivals* edited by Andrew Fusek Peters (ISBN 978-0-7502-5568-4)
Approximate Duration:	Two weeks

Big Picture

During this sequence, children will listen to the poem 'The Big Steel Band' and discuss its subject, rhythmic sounds and rhyming language as a group. Through a range of supportive activities, the children will have the opportunity to explore carnivals and festivals in more depth.

Phonics Focuses

The children will look at sounds and words related to the graphemes 'oa', 'ee' and 'er', as well as developing skills in recognising letter sounds and rhyming spelling patterns for CVC and CVCC words. They will also revisit recognising syllable beats in one- and two-syllable words.

Learning Outcomes: See 'Learning Outcomes' Chart, on pages xi–xiv.

Key Vocabulary: carnival, sunshine sound, steel band, costumed, float

Home Links

Encourage children to:
- ask family members about their own experiences of parades, carnivals and festivals
- use simple instruments or household objects to create a marching beat
- share any photographs or other images of festivals, carnivals or parades they have attended.

Resources Required

Workbook Pages: 20–22, 28

Resource Sheets 16.1–16.2: Carnival Float Card; My Carnival

General Resources:
- Recorded steel-band music, or internet access and speakers
- Craft paper
- A selection of percussion instruments
- Two boxes
- A bag
- Craft materials (e.g. scissors, glue, coloured pens and pencils, fabric, string, patterned/coloured paper, newspaper, tape, glue, paint, empty boxes, cardboard)
- A selection of fancy-dress outfits and accessories (e.g. cloth, masks, streamer batons)
- Simple games equipment such as soft balls, skittles, bean bags and hoops

Background Knowledge

Explain to the children that:
- carnivals, festivals and processions are community celebrations often connected with religious, cultural or historical events
- steel band performers play steel pans, which were invented in the 1930s, in Trinidad and Tobago
- steel pans were originally oil barrels moulded to make musical notes and sounds
- steel pans are played like drums, with straight, rubber-ended sticks.

Performance Ideas and Storytelling Suggestions

- ★ Read through the poem out loud to yourself before performing it to the class, to help you decide where to add emphasis and intonation to key words or lines.
- ★ Read the last, repetitive phrase of each stanza slowly, so the children can hear it clearly and note the repetition and the 'sunshine sound' description.
- ★ Use hand actions (see the 'The Big Steel Band' text on **Connect**). Practise and learn these before performing them to the children.
- ★ If possible, play steel-band music during the poem, softly while you speak and loudly at the end of each verse. (Video recordings of steel-band music are available for free online.)

Sequence Structure

This chart offers suggestions on the order and timings of exploring the story over a two-week period. However, please feel free to adapt the sessions to your own planning and suitable timings for your whole class or set groups.

Exploring the Poem

Tip: If possible, aim to perform the poem to or with the children regularly over the two-week period, or before any related activity, so that the children get to know the poem and its meaning well.

WEEK 1 (PHASE 1)	WEEKS 1–2 (PHASE 2)	WEEK 2 (PHASE 3)
Introduction to the poem	**Getting to know the poem**	**Performing the poem**
All sections could be done in one session or split over two or three sessions.	Aim to hold one or two sessions on getting to know the poem, each retelling the poem and then including your own choice of activities.	These sessions could be rehearsed and performed at different times across the week.
1. **What do we know?** (approx. 15 minutes) 2. **Let's listen and talk** (approx. 20 minutes) **Extra consolidation activity:** • Listening to the steel band (20–25 minutes)	3. **Let's get to know the poem** (10–15 minutes) **'Structure focus' activity:** • A new verse (approx. 20 minutes) **'Vocabulary focus' activities:** • Rhyming carnival floats (approx. 20 minutes) • Finding action words (approx. 15 minutes) **'Phonics focus' activity:** • Syllable beats • (15–20 minutes)	4. **Let's put on a performance** (30–40 minutes)

Literacy Activities

READING	WRITING	PHONICS WORK
• Matching floats • Letter floats	• Steel-pan spelling • Carnival comic strips	• 'oa' words • 'er' and 'ee' stalls

Cross-curricular Activities

Adult-led activities:
- Creating a class float (Expressive Arts; Understanding the World)
- Festival music (Expressive Arts; Physical Education; Understanding the World)
- Carnival-stall games (Mathematics; PSHE; Physical Development)

Child-led activities:
- Festival fancy dress (Expressive Arts; Communication and Language)
- Making floats (Expressive Arts; Understanding the World)
- Role-play carnival stalls (Communication and Language)

Sequence Assessment

- Communication and Language
- Reading
- Writing
- Review of the Big Picture

EXPLORING THE POEM

PHASE 1: Introduction to the poem

Session 1: What do we know?

Play the children some steel-band music, and use an online video-hosting website to show them a video of a carnival parade (for example, the Mardi Gras procession in New Orleans). Discuss what is going on in the video, introducing appropriate vocabulary for different parts of the procession (for example, 'floats', 'parade', 'musicians', 'dancers').

Then give prompts and ask open questions to assess the children's current knowledge of festivals, carnivals and parades. For example:

- *Have you ever seen or been part of a carnival or parade?*
- *What did you do there?*
- *Were there different floats?*

- *How did the people dress up?*
- *What were people doing as the procession went by? (For example cheering, waving)*
- *What kind of music was involved?*
- *Have you ever heard a steel band play?*

Discuss the **Background Knowledge** given above. Explain to the children that they are going to listen to a poem about a carnival procession that has a steel band, and do lots of fun activities about carnivals.

Session 2: Let's listen and talk

Play the children the steel-band music again, and remind them briefly of their discussion from the previous session.

Show the **Storyteller** video for 'The Big Steel Band' on **Connect**, or read and perform it yourself (see the **Performance Ideas and Storytelling Suggestions** above).

After the reading, check that the children understand any new or difficult words (see **Key Vocabulary** above).

Ask questions to check the children's understanding of the poem. These can be open to group discussion or children can pair with talk partners before reporting back to the group. For example:

- *How do the people use their hands and feet when they hear the music?*

- *What pass by all day?*
- *How do the people in costume move to the music?*
- *What do they see that begins with 'k'?*
- *What is with the king?*
- *What makes a 'sunshine sound'?*

Say the poem one more time, encouraging the children to join in with (parts of) the verses' repeated final line.

Extra consolidation activity

Listening to the steel band

- Play the steel-band music again, and encourage the children to move and sway to the musical beat.
- Remind the children of the verses' repeated final line.
- Ask talk partners to discuss what the poet means by a 'sunshine sound' before feeding back to the class. (The steel drums make a bright, cheerful, warm sound.)
- Ask talk partners to come up with one other word they could use to describe the sound and then discuss these as a class.

EXPLORING THE POEM

PHASE 2: Getting to know the poem

Session 3: Let's get to know the poem 👥👥 👥👥

Play the children the steel-band music again, and remind them of the poem. Ask them what they remember about it. Retell the poem using the **Storyteller** video on **Connect**, or by displaying the poem and reading it aloud to the class. Then retell the poem again, asking the children to join in with the actions described (such as 'clap our hands', 'stamp our feet', 'swing and sway' and 'wave'), and with (parts of) the verses' repeated final line.

After the retelling, choose focus activities to explore the poem in more depth.

'Structure focus' activity

A new verse 👥👥 👥👥

- Display the interactive activity "The Big Steel Band' New Verse', and explain to the children that they are going to help you write a new verse for the poem.
- Look at the writing frame. On each line, there is one word describing an action taken that you need to select.
- Click to reveal the three options for each missing word. Work with the children to choose one of the options for each gap.
- Read out the final verse with the children. Note again that the last line, about the steel band, is always the same.

'Vocabulary focus' activities

Rhyming carnival floats 👥👥 👥👥

- Write the eight rhyming words from the poem onto copies of Resource Sheet 16.1: 'street', 'feet', 'hands', 'band', 'day', 'sway', 'king' and 'sing'.
- Mix up the word floats and display them. Explain that the rhyming pairs need to be matched up again.
- Model one pairing, selecting 'street', and read through the other words to hear which one rhymes. Select 'feet' and then sound and blend the words, noting that both words end in 'eet'.
- Work with the children in the same way, finding the rhyming pairs and putting them next to each other.
- Finally, make a float procession by asking the children to help you put the rhyming pairs into the order they appear in the poem.

Finding action words 👥👥 👥👥

- Display the interactive activity 'Finding Action Words'.
- Read out the list of different action words with the children, sounding out and blending words that the children may be able to read (such as 'clap', 'stamp', 'swing' and 'sing').
- Ask the children to choose and drag the action words that are used in the poem into the balloons.
- Discuss whether they think the other action words could be used in the poem.

'Phonics focus' activity

Syllable beats 👥👥 👥👥

- Give the children a collection of percussion instruments (or let them clap their hands and stamp their feet).
- Read out a selection of one-syllable words (for example, 'king', 'band', 'sway', feet'), clapping the single syllable beat.
- Ask the children to follow you, using their instruments (or hands or feet). Say each word four times.
- Move onto two-syllable words (for example, 'sunshine', 'dragon'), and again, ask the children to make the syllable beats.
- Finally, say and repeat the three-syllable word 'carnival', again asking the children to make the syllable beats.

EXPLORING THE POEM

PHASE 3: Performing the poem

Session 4: Let's put on a performance

Over the week, encourage the children to explore the poem through role-play by asking them to move like people at the carnival procession:

- Play steel-band music and encourage the children to enjoy and move to it. Suggest movements from the poem (such as clapping, stamping, swinging and swaying) before adding other movements (such as skipping, wiggling or jumping).
- Play the music softly and then loudly, asking the children to match their everyday movements to the volume. They should move more quickly when the music is loud, and slow down as it is quietened.
- Create a conga line, asking the children to hold onto each other and follow you around the room to music.

During the final session, remind the children of their work so far. Show the poem again using the **Storyteller** video on **Connect**, or retell it with the children from the whiteboard. Then ask the children to work together to create a performance of the poem.

- Put the children into four groups: steel-band musicians, people on floats, people dancing in the procession and bystanders.
- Discuss what each group should do during the procession, using the poem for guidance if necessary.
- As you read out the first verse of the poem, set off the procession with the steel-band group miming their actions to music.
- Follow this with people waving from floats (in costumes if available) and dancers moving and swaying, during the second verse.
- Finally, during the third verse, and the bystanders should cheer and wave, and point to things on the floats.
- If time allows, permit the children to try out each different group.
- Encourage all children to join in with creating a rhythmic beat for the poem, and to join in with the repeated line if they can.
- If possible, film the performance for the children to watch and enjoy.

Differentiation: More confident readers may wish to assist you in reading out the poem.

LITERACY ACTIVITIES

Reading

Matching floats

- Ask mixed-ability pairs to work on the interactive activity 'Match the Float Banner', matching the banners to the correct carnival floats.

Differentiation: Ask more confident readers to write their own banners for a float. What would they like to see on a float, and what would the banners say? Less confident readers can do this orally and attempt to write at least some of the words with support.

Letter floats

- Show the children a copy of Resource Sheet 16.1 with the letter 'P' written on it.
- Ask them to help you think of people, animals or things starting with 'p' that could travel on the float (for example, pans, a princess, a puppy, packets, pens, a pilot). Emphasise the /p/ sound each time.
- Collect as many 'p' words as you can before repeating these steps with a different letter.

Writing

Steel-pan spelling

- Ask mixed-ability pairs to work on the interactive activity 'Steel-Pan Spelling', dragging steel pans showing graphemes into order to make up a word.

Differentiation: Ask more confident writers to write simple sentences using their created words. Less confident writers could focus on spelling skills for words that have similar patterns and sounds.

Carnival comic strips

- Hand out copies of Resource Sheet 16.2.
- Ask the children to look at the images and sentences in turn and ask them what they are.
- Read out each sentence and ask what the missing initial letter is. Let them write it in.
- Then ask them to colour in the images.
- Cut out the images with sentences for the children to stick down on craft paper in a procession order of their own choice.

Differentiation: Ask more confident writers to write other sentences and draw more images for extra sections of the procession. Support less confident writers to use blend taught sounds and access key word prompts so that they work towards writing words and sentence making too.

Phonics Work

'oa' words

- Ask mixed-ability pairs to work on the interactive activity 'Float 'oa' Words', matching the images to the correct 'oa' words.
- Then ask the children to sound and blend each 'oa' word.

Differentiation: Support less confident writers by segmenting each letter and 'oa' grapheme. Show an image to all children, and ask them to write out the 'oa' word it represents. More confident writers should attempt to write out the word independently. Assess how they sound out and segment the word for spelling.

'er' and 'ee' stalls

- Make a set of eight word cards for words ending in 'er' (for example, 'hammer', 'banner', 'letter', 'summer', 'boxer', 'dinner', 'singer' and 'digger').
- Make a set of eight word cards for words containing 'ee' (for example, 'see', 'eel', 'keep', 'weep', 'feet', 'deep', 'meet' and 'feel').
- Put out two boxes labelled 'er' and 'ee'.
- Hold up an 'er' card and read it out. Note that the 'er' is at the end of the word. Model putting it into the 'er' box.
- Hold up an 'ee' card and read it out. Model putting it into the 'ee' box.
- Ask a child to take a card, read the word and say the sound for 'er' or 'ee'.
- They should then put the card into the correct box.
- Repeat these steps until all the cards are sorted.

CROSS-CURRICULAR ACTIVITIES

Adult-led activities 👥👤

Creating a class float (Expressive Arts; Understanding the World)

- Designate a space for the children to help create a class float.
- Work with the children to decide what theme they would like their float to have (for example, mini-beasts, space, a jungle), how it could be decorated and what props would be needed.
- Set up various small sessions for the children to produce materials for the float and help to put it together.

Festival music (Expressive Arts; Physical Education; Understanding the World)

- Set up times when the children can experiment trying out different classroom objects as percussion instruments to accompany different types of music.
- Encourage them to dance and move freely to their music.

Carnival-stall games (Mathematics; PSHE; Physical Development)

Organise fair-stall games for the children to play. Ideas could include:
- rolling a ball at skittles
- throwing bean bags at a target
- guessing how many objects are in a jar
- throwing hoops over objects.

Popcorn fun (Expressive Arts)

- If you have the equipment, make some popcorn with the children.
- Discuss the changes that happen from the kernels to the full-blown popcorn.
- Decorate popcorn paper bags or use it for a textural effect in art work.

Child-led activities 👥👤 👥 👤

Festival fancy dress (Expressive Arts; Communication and Language)

- Provide a range of fancy-dress outfits and accessories.
- Encourage the children to dress up in the theme of a class topic, during their own games and/or when using the class float (see above).

Making floats (Expressive Arts; Understanding the World)

- Ask the children to design and decorate mini floats using their own themes and ideas.
- Then use a craft session to ask the children to create their floats, using either Resource Sheet 16.1 or empty boxes.
- Display the floats, linking them with a piece of string to show the procession.

Role-play carnival stalls (Communication and Language)

- Create two or three carnival stalls, either to sell object or to host games (see **Carnival-stall games**, above).
- Encourage the children to take turns being the stall owners and customers.

Differentiation: More confident children may be able to use small denominations of money (for example, pennies) to perform simple sums at the stalls. All children could join in with the role play use of coins, learning from more confident children modelling first.

SEQUENCE ASSESSMENT

Communication and Language

- Does the child join in with and recognise repeated refrains, and anticipate the end phrase in a poem?
- Has the child extended their vocabulary by exploring the meanings and sounds of new words?
- Does the child use talk to organise, sequence and clarify thinking and ideas about the poem?
- Does the child use intonation, rhythm and phrasing to make their meaning clear to others?
- Does the child use language to imagine and recreate roles and experiences in play situations?

Reading

- Can the child recognise rhythm in the poem's verses?
- Can the child anticipate key words and rhymes in the poem?
- Can the child hear initial sounds for words?
- Can the child segment and blend sounds in CVC/CVCC words?
- Can the child recognise the sounds for the graphemes 'oa', 'er' and 'ee'?
- Can the child read simple sentences?

Writing

- Can the child segment and blend sounds in CVC/CVCC words?
- Can the child use some clearly identifiable letters to communicate meaning, representing some sounds correctly and in sequence?
- Can the child begin to write labels and words for captions?
- Can the child write simple sentences?

Review of the Big Picture

At the end of this sequence, discuss with the children what they liked about the poem. Ask: *Do you think this was a fun and happy day? What word described the happy sound of the steel band? Which part of the procession would you like to have seen? What rhyming words can you remember?*

Encourage each child to show and explain examples of their writing and reading achievements, and any cross-curricular activities they enjoyed.

Use the 'Pupil observation chart' to record each child's responses and attainment.

SEQUENCE 17 Our World: A Tale from Another Country

TERM 3 (SUMMER): 2nd half term

Main Topic:	Our World
Subtopic:	A Tale from Another Country
Text Type:	Story
Main Source Text:	*Mama Panya's Pancakes* by Mary and Rich Chamberlin (ISBN 978-1-905-23663-3)
Approximate Duration:	Two weeks

Big Picture

During this sequence, children will listen to the story 'Mama Panya's Pancakes' and discuss its messages, main characters, events and vocabulary as a group.

A range of supportive activities will also give the children an opportunity to explore the story in more detail, and to find out more about Kenya, its country of origin.

Phonics Focuses

The children will look at sounds and words related to the graphemes 'er' and 'oi', as well as practising recognising tricky words. They will also develop their skills in segmenting words and blending sounds.

Learning Outcomes: See 'Learning Outcomes' Chart, on pages xi–xiv.

Key Vocabulary: baobab tree, thighs, plaintain, pepper, drinking-gourds, cardamom spice, thumb piano

Home Links

Encourage children to:
- find out more about rural life in Kenya
- make pancakes with different fillings
- perform conscious acts of kindness or friendship.

Resources Required

Workbook Pages: 15–16, 25–26, 28

Resource Sheets 17.1–17.3: Kiswahili Words; Story Object Labels; Mama Panya's Pancakes

General Resources:

- A world map
- Craft paper
- Craft materials (e.g. paint, straw, cardboard, glitter, fabric, coloured pens and pencils, coloured chalk, patterned/coloured paper, newspaper, tape, glue)
- A puppet (or small-world toy person)
- A green chilli pepper, or an image of a chilli pepper
- Small-world toys (e.g. people and animals)
- Equipment and ingredients for pancakes (see Resource Sheet 17.3)

Background Knowledge

Explain to the children that:
- the story is set in Kenya, which is a country in Africa
- Africa is a continent that is found south of Europe. It is mostly very hot
- many people who live in Kenyan villages are farmers – they help to grow crops or look after animals. At markets, they sell the things they have to spare, and buy the things they need
- the main languages spoken in Kenya are English and Kiswahili (also called Swahili). There are some Kiswahili words in the story (see Resource Sheet 17.1).

Performance ideas and storytelling suggestions

- ★ Read through the story out loud to yourself before reading it to the class, to help you decide where you could add emphasis and intonation to key words or lines.
- ★ Read each page slowly, with extra emphasis on the repetitive phrases.
- ★ Refer to Resource Sheet 17.1 for the correct pronunciations and translations of the Kiswahili words in the story.
- ★ When you reach a Kiswahili phrase or word, as the children to guess what it means based on context, and then explain the translation to them.

Sequence Structure

This chart offers suggestions on the order and timings of exploring the story over a two-week period. However, please feel free to adapt the sessions to your own planning and suitable timings for your whole class or set groups.

Exploring the Story

Tip: If possible, aim to read or show the story to the children regularly over the two-week period, or before any related activity, so that the children get to know the story and its messages well.

WEEK 1 (PHASE 1)	WEEKS 1–2 (PHASE 2)	WEEK 1-2 (PHASE 3)
Introduction to the story	**Getting to know the story**	**Performing the story**
All sections could be done in one session or split over two or three sessions.	Aim to hold one or two sessions on getting to know the story, each retelling the story and then including your own choice of activities.	Aim to hold one or two sessions at different times across the two-week period.
1. **What do we know?** (20–25 minutes) 2. **Let's listen and talk** (approx. 20 minutes) **Extra consolidation activity:** ● An act of kindness (20–25 minutes)	3. **Let's get to know the story** (10–15 minutes) **'Structure focus' activities:** ● On the way to market (20–25 minutes) ● Who bought what? (approx. 15 minutes) **'Vocabulary focus' activity:** ● Kiswahili words (approx. 10 minutes) **'Phonics focus' activity:** ● Baobab-tree '–er' words (approx. 20 minutes)	4. **Let's put on a performance** (30–40 minutes)

Literacy Activities

READING	WRITING	PHONICS WORK
● Making pancakes	● A little bit and a little bit more	● Word pancakes
● Story objects	● Thank-you notes	● Find the coins

Cross-curricular Activities

Adult-led activities:
● Making pancakes (Expressive Arts; Understanding the World; PSHE)
● Kenyan village models (Expressive Arts; Understanding the World)
● Kenya and the UK (Understanding the world; Communication and Language)

Child-led activities:
● A Kenyan corner (Communication and Language; Understanding the World)
● Kenyan patterns (Mathematics; Expressive Arts)
● The Kenyan flag (Understanding the world)

Sequence Assessment

● Communication and Language
● Reading
● Writing
● Review of the Big Picture

EXPLORING THE STORY

PHASE 1: Introduction to the story

Session 1: What do we know?

Show the children a world map and point to your location. Then point to Kenya. Give prompts and ask open questions to assess the children's current knowledge about Kenya. For example:

- *In what continent in Kenya?*
- *Has anyone ever been to Africa?*
- *What do you think the weather is usually like there?*

Discuss the **Background Knowledge** given above, and discuss ways that life in a Kenyan village differs from life where you are. Then explain to the children that they are going to listen to a story about a woman and her son who live in a Kenyan village, and do lots of fun activities about Kenya and the story.

Session 2: Let's listen and talk

Show the children Kenya on the world map again, and remind them briefly of their discussion from the previous session.

Show the **Storyteller** video for 'Mama Panya's Pancakes' on **Connect**, or read the story yourself (see the **Performance Ideas and Storytelling Suggestions** above).

After the reading, check that the children understand any new or difficult words (see **Key Vocabulary** above).

Ask questions to check the children's understanding of the story. These can be open to group discussion or children can pair with talk partners before reporting back to the group. For example:

- *Where were Mama Panya and Adika going?*
- *How many coins did Mama have?*

- *What was Mzee Odolo doing when Adika invited him to eat pancakes?*
- *What animals were Sawandi and Naiman looking after?*
- *How did Adika get the plumpest pepper in the market?*
- *Why did Adika and Mama's friends bring extra food to the pancake feast?*
- *Where did everyone eat the pancakes?*

Finally, ask the children to share their own experiences of cooking or eating pancakes. Note that pancakes can be sweet or savoury, and wrapped around all types of food.

Extra consolidation activity

An act of kindness

- Ask the children to sit in a circle.
- Discuss with them in what way Adika was kind to his friends and neighbours. (He invited them to join him and his mother for pancakes, when they didn't have a lot to share.)
- Then discuss how this kindness was rewarded: each of the guests brought a little extra gift, and this made the pancake party special.
- Ask each child to think of something kind that they could do for others, moving around the circle.
- Praise all the children and emphasise how good they would feel by doing the act of kindness.

EXPLORING THE STORY

PHASE 2: Getting to know the story

Session 3: Let's get to know the story 👥 👥

Point to Kenya on the world map again, and remind the children of the story. Ask them what they remember about it. Retell the story using the **Storyteller** video on **Connect**, or read the story yourself. Encourage the children to join in with the repetitive phrases (for example, 'one step ahead' and 'a little bit and a little bit more').

After the retelling, choose focus activities to explore the story in more depth.

'Structure focus' activities

On the way to market 👥 👥

- Create a story-map display using craft materials, to help the children retell the story in sequence order. Show the settings of the village, baobab tree, river, cattle field and market.
- Ask the children to add features such as Mama Panya's hut and the market stalls.
- Move a puppet or small-world toy along the settings, asking the children to retell the events of the story.

Who brought what? 👥 👥

- Display the interactive activity 'Who Brought What?'.
- Read out the names of the characters and the list of things brought to the pancake party.
- Ask: *Who brought what to the pancake party?*
- Encourage the children to help you to link the characters and their gifts.
- If they need help, remind the children where Mama Panya and Adika met each character.

'Vocabulary focus' activity

Kiswahili words 👥 👥

- Use Resource Sheet 17.1 to focus the children's attention on the Kiswahili words in the story. Find the words in the story to place them in context.
- Over the two weeks, encourage the children to join you in using some of the simpler words, for example, by greeting each other with 'jambo' or thanking each other with 'asante sana'.

'Phonics focus' activity

Baobab-tree '–er' words 👥 👥

- Prepare eight word cards from craft paper (perhaps cut to resemble leaves) showing the words 'pepper', 'supper', 'butter', 'seller', 'summer', 'cattle', 'flour' and 'mama'.
- Draw a large baobab tree, with five branches, on craft paper.
- Show the children a pepper (or a picture of one) and ask if they know what it is called. Refer to the pepper bought at the market in the story.
- Show the 'pepper' word card and sound out the word.
- Underline the 'er' and ask the children make its sound. Add the word card to the end of a baobab branch.
- Display and read out the other word cards. Ask the children to identify the '–er' words.
- Underline the –er in each case and add these word cards to the other baobab branches.

EXPLORING THE STORY

PHASE 3: Performing the story

Session 4: Let's put on a performance 👥 👥

Over the two weeks, encourage the children to explore the story through role-play. For example:

- Ask the children to role-play having a pancake feast, miming cooking the pancakes over an imaginary stove and then sitting down in a big circle to eat. Encourage any children who may want to also entertain the group as they eat.

- Suggest that different groups role-play the different characters Mama Panya and Adiki meet, miming fishing, herding cattle or selling goods in a market. In each case, encourage them to think about the people doing these tasks. Ask: *Where and how do they live? Why are they doing what they do?*

During the final session, remind the children of their work so far. Show the story again using the **Storyteller** video on **Connect**, or retell it with the children from the whiteboard. Then ask the children to work together to act out the story.

- Set up the room so that the children can make the journey to the market, adding area markers representing Mama Panya's hut, the baobab tree, the river, the cattle field and the market (with a plantain stand, flour stand and spice table).

- Put the children into groups representing each character met by Mama Panya after she leaves her village: Adiki by the tree, Mzee Odolo by the river, Sawandi and Naiman with their cattle, Gamila selling plantains, Biba and Bwana Zawenna selling flour and Rafiki Kaya selling spices.

- Station each group along the journey.

- Acting as Mama Panya, clap to create a walking beat and start your journey.

- Once you have 'collected' the Adiki group, encourage the children with you at each stage to invite the next person-group to eat pancakes with you.

- After each group is collected, ask the children: *How many people have you asked back for pancakes? How will we have enough?*

- Encourage the children to reply: *We have a little bit, and a little bit more!*

- Ensure that all groups come together to celebrate at the end of the story.

LITERACY ACTIVITIES

Reading

Making pancakes

- Ask mixed-ability pairs to work on the interactive activity, 'Making Pancakes', selecting the correct ingredients.
- Ask the children to explain their choices.

Differentiation: More confident children could go on to discuss how Mama Panya made the pancakes, using the correct sequence and perhaps referring to Resource Sheet 17.3.

Story objects

- Print copies of Resource Sheet 17.2, cut out the word labels and hand one set, plus the object image board, to talk partners.
- Ask the children to select a word card at random, and read out the word before they match it to the correct image.
- Repeat these steps, until all the cards are placed.

Differentiation: Suggest that more confident readers use a board and set of word cards each, and compete to see who can read and place the words first.

Writing

A little bit and a little bit more

- Ask mixed-ability pairs to work on the interactive activity 'A Little Bit and a Little Bit More', placing the final letters to create new words.
- Once the children have completed the activity, ask them which of the four pictures is the odd one out. (The robin, as they are not found in Kenya.)

Differentiation: Encourage less confident writers to say the four groups of missing letters out loud and try sounding them out at the end of each word, to see which one makes sense.

Thank-you notes

- Ask the children to write a short thank-you note from one of the story characters to Adika and Mama Panya for their pancake feast.
- Orally compose what a character would write, with help from the children (for example, 'To Adika and Mama, Thank you for the good pancakes. From _____').
- Write out the sentence, asking the children to help you spell the words. Then write out the names of the characters, so the children can chose whose thank-you note they are writing.
- Ask the children to copy the sentence out, adding one of the names.
- If time allows, encourage the children to decorate their notes using craft materials.

Differentiation: Encourage more confident writers to write their own sentences with minimal support.

Phonics Work

Word pancakes

Use this activity to enhance the children's skills at recognising a tricky word:

- Ask mixed-ability pairs to work on the interactive activity 'Word Pancakes', identifying the tricky words.
- Then encourage the children to work out how to read these words by sounding out known sounds.

Find the coins

- Make a set of craft-paper coins showing the words 'coin', 'oil', 'boil', 'coil', 'join' and 'soil'.
- Hide the coins, and ask the children to find them.
- Once the coins have been found, select a coin, say the word and then underline the 'oi'. Sound this out, and ask the children to copy you.
- Then ask the children to sound out and blend the 'oi' words on the rest of the coins.
- Ask talk partners to compose oral sentences using the words, to reinforce word comprehension.

Differentiation: Encourage more confident children to think of other 'oi' words and write them on extra blank coins.

CROSS-CURRICULAR ACTIVITIES

Adult-led activities 👥👤

Making pancakes (Expressive Arts; Understanding the World; PSHE)

- If possible, use Resource Sheet 17.3 to prepare the pancake mix with the children and allow them to watch you cooking pancakes. (You could alternatively prepare some pancakes in advance, as they can be eaten cold.)
- Remind the children that, in Kenya as in many places around the world, the pancakes are made thin, and wrapped around sweet or savoury fillings.
- Set out a selection of sweet and savoury fillings (for example, jam, banana, chocolate spread, cheese, tuna and salad) for the children to try when they eat the pancakes.

Kenyan village models (Expressive Arts; Understanding the World)

- Search online to find some images of Kenyan huts and display them.
- Ask the children to use craft materials to make model Kenyan huts like those in the story, ensuring they paint the huts colourfully, and assisting them with any cutting and sticking.
- Ideas include large, cut down cardboard tubes for the round walls and straw stuck onto card cones for roofs. Make sure the children paint the huts and add colourful doors. If they are to be used as part of a story display, let the children also create market stalls from card and use modelling clay for the produce.
- Invite the children to use these villages with small-world toys in their play.

Kenya and the UK (Understanding the World; Communication and Language)

- Ask the children to look at specific books in the school library or specific pages online to find more facts or stories about Kenya.
- Ask groups to discuss the differences between Kenya and the UK.
- Display what they have found in a designated classroom area.

Making thumb pianos (Understanding the World; Expressive Arts)

- Make thumb pianos, by cutting out small squares of wood and letting the children paint patterns or the colours of the Kenyan flag.
- Once dry, use masking tape to hold in place one end of a set of hair grips with the other ends bent up to make the sound. Let the children use them along with drums to make African beats.

Child-led activities 👥👤 👤👤 👤

A Kenyan corner (Communication and Language; Understanding the World)

- Designate a play space to represent a Kenyan hut, adding simple furniture and bright cloth.
- Encourage the children use it for imaginative play, and to retell the story using their own words.
- They could also set up a market area where the children can play at selling and buying.
- Encourage the children to take turns being the stall owners and customers.

Differentiation: More confident children may be able to use small denominations of money (for example, pennies) to perform simple sums at the stalls. All children could join in with the role play use of coins.

Kenyan patterns (Mathematics; Expressive Arts)

- Search online for 'Kenyan patterns' and display them.
- Ask groups to look at the patterns and discuss them. What shapes can they see and name?
- Encourage the children to use shape templates to create their own patterns.

The Kenyan flag (Understanding the World)

- Search online for images of the Kenyan flag and display them.
- Ask the children to draw and paint or colour in the flag accurately.
- Display them around the room.

SEQUENCE ASSESSMENT

Communication and Language
- Does the child use language to imagine and recreate roles and experiences in play situations?
- Does the child introduce and explore the story in their play?
- Does the child listen and respond to ideas expressed by others in conversation or discussion?
- Does the child use talk to organise, sequence and clarify thinking and ideas about the story?

Reading
- Can the child describe the main settings, events and characters of the story?
- Can the child hear and say the sounds for the graphemes 'er' and 'oi'?
- Can the child segment the sounds in simple words and blend them together?
- Can the child begin to read words and simple sentences?
- Does the child know that information can also be retrieved from books and computers?

Writing
- Can the child segment and blend sounds for words and write them down?
- Can the child recognise the sounds for the graphemes 'er' and 'oi'?
- Can the child write their own name and simple labels and captions?
- Can the child attempt to write short sentences?

Review of the Big Picture
At the end of this sequence, discuss with the children what happened in the story and in what order. Ask: *What was your favourite part of the story? Why did Adika's friends bring extra food for the pancake party? What phrases were often repeated?*

Encourage each child to show and explain examples of their writing and reading achievements, and any cross-curricular activities they enjoyed.

Use the 'Pupil observation chart' to record each child's responses and attainment.

SEQUENCE 18 Our World: Holiday Experiences

TERM 3 (SUMMER) 2nd half term

Main Topic:	Our World
Subtopic:	Holiday Experiences
Text Type:	Poem
Main Source Text:	'Holiday Memories' by June Crebbin, from *The Puffin Book of Fantastic First Poems* edited by June Crebbin (ISBN 978-0-141-30898-2)
Approximate Duration:	Two weeks

Big Picture
During this sequence, children will listen to the poem 'Holiday Memories' and explore the places, characters and actions it describes, as well as its rhythmic sound and rhyming language.

Through a range of supportive activities, the children will also have the opportunity to explore holiday activities and trips in more depth.

Phonics Focuses
The children will look at sounds and words related to the graphemes 'oo', 'or' and 'ear'. They will also look at longer words using 'ck', as well as developing skills in recognising letter sounds and rhyming patterns.

Learning Outcomes: See 'Learning Outcomes' Chart, on pages xi–xiv.

Key Vocabulary: Timbuktu, wrestle, jaguar, moonbeam, gossip, Greyhound bus, grapple, Grizzly

Home Links
Encourage children to:
- ask friends of family members to share past holiday memories
- find photos or souvenirs of past holidays
- think about what they would most like to do over the summer holidays.

Resources Required
Workbook Pages: 17–18, 21–22, 28–30

Resource Sheets 18.1–18.2: Holiday Sentences; My Holiday Postcard

General Resources:
- A holiday postcard or brochure
- Two small suitcases (or cardboard boxes decorated to look like suitcases)
- Craft materials (e.g. thick cardboard, paint, glitter, fabric, coloured pens and pencils, coloured chalk, patterned/coloured paper, newspaper, tape, glue)
- Craft paper
- Classroom objects or craft materials to represent words containing the letters 'ck' (e.g. a toy duck, small truck, giraffe toy with a long neck, some black fabric and a stick)
- A rucksack
- A scrapbook for each child (perhaps simply made from folded craft paper)

Background Knowledge
Explain to the children that:
- the holiday 'memories' in the poem are intended to be fantastical and over the top, as if the narrator is imagining them or getting carried away and showing off
- there are lots of different kinds of holidays – going abroad and seeing extraordinary things is one option, but many of the best holidays involve simple activities, staying close to home, and spending time with family and friends.

Performance ideas and storytelling suggestions
- ★ Read through the poem out loud to yourself before performing it to the class, to help you decide where to add emphasis and intonation to key words or lines (for example, the rhyming words).
- ★ Say the last two words of the poem ('THE END') loudly and with strong emphasis.
- ★ Use hand actions (see the 'Holiday Memories' text on **Connect**). Practise and learn these before performing them to the children.

Sequence Structure

This chart offers suggestions on the order and timings of exploring the story over a two-week period. However, please feel free to adapt the sessions to your own planning and suitable timings for your whole class or set groups.

Exploring the Poem

Tip: If possible, aim to perform the poem to or with the children regularly over the two-week period, or before any related activity, so that the children get to know the poem and its meaning well.

WEEK 1 (PHASE 1)	WEEKS 1–2 (PHASE 2)	WEEK 2 (PHASE 3)
Introduction to the poem	**Getting to know the poem**	**Performing the poem**
All sections could be done in one session or split over two or three sessions.	Aim to hold one or two sessions on getting to know the poem, each retelling the poem and then including your own choice of activities.	These sessions could be rehearsed and performed at different times across the week.
1. **What do we know?** (approx. 15 minutes) 2. **Let's listen and talk** (approx. 20 minutes) **Extra consolidation activity:** ● Holiday memories in detail (approx. 20 minutes)	3. **Let's get to know the poem** (10–15 minutes) **'Structure focus' activities:** ● More holiday 'memories' (20–25 minutes) ● What did I do? (approx. 15 minutes) **'Vocabulary focus' activity:** ● Holiday photo labels (approx. 15 minutes) **'Phonics focus' activity** ● 'oo' and 'or' suitcase sounds (15–20 minutes)	4. **Let's put on a performance** (30–40 minutes)

Literacy Activities

READING	WRITING	PHONICS WORK
● Holiday sentences ● Holiday transport	● Postcard sentences ● Writing labels	● Finding 'ear' words ● Rucksack words

Cross-curricular Activities

Adult-led activities:
- My holiday scrapbook (Expressive Arts; PSHE)
- Holiday pictures (Expressive Arts; Communication and Language)
- Model transport (Expressive Arts; Understanding the World)

Child-led activities:
- Packing my case (Communication and Language; Understanding the World)
- Tickets and passengers (Communication and Language; PSHE)
- Different settings (Communication and Language; Understanding the World)
- Picture montage (PSHE; Communication and Language)

Sequence Assessment

- Communication and Language
- Reading
- Writing
- Review of the Big Picture

EXPLORING THE POEM

PHASE 1: Introduction to the poem

Session 1: What do we know?

Show the children the holiday postcard or brochure. Give prompts and ask open questions to encourage the children to share their thoughts on holidays. For example:

- *Where would you most like to go on holiday?*
- *What or who would you like to see?*
- *How would you travel?*
- *Who would go with you?*

Discuss the **Background Knowledge** given above, and tell the children one of your own favourite holiday memories. Ask talk partners to share the things they remember most fondly about any holidays they have had, before they feed back to the class.

Then explain to the children that they are going to listen to a poem called 'Holiday Memories', and do lots of fun activities about memories and going on holiday.

Session 2: Let's listen and talk

Show the children the holiday postcard or brochure again, and remind them briefly of their discussion from the previous session.

Show the **Storyteller** video for 'Holiday Memories' on **Connect**, or read and perform it yourself (see the **Performance Ideas and Storytelling Suggestions** above).

After the reading, check that the children understand any new or difficult words (see **Key Vocabulary** above).

Ask questions to check the children's understanding of the story. These can be open to group discussion or children can pair with talk partners before reporting back to the group. For example:

- *Where did the narrator see a kangaroo?*
- *What did they swim?*

- *With what bird did they chat?*
- *What did they do to the stars?*
- *How did they travel across the desert?*
- *Who did they hear singing?*
- *Who did they chase round the bend?*

Finally, ask the children if they think anyone could really do these things on holiday, and discuss why the narrator says they happened.

Extra consolidation activity

Holiday memories in detail

- Point out again that the poem's narrator is not describing a normal holiday trip.
- Look at examples that make this clear (for example, the narrator describes talking to animals, going into space and listening to mermaids).
- Allocate an activity from the poem to each pair of talk partners.
- Ask them to imagine that they are doing this activity, discussing what they can see, hear and feel in more detail. Ask questions to guide them if necessary (for example, *What did the mermaid sing? Was it good? What did she look like?*).
- Then ask the pairs to feed back their discussion to the class.

EXPLORING THE POEM

PHASE 2: Getting to know the poem

Session 3: Let's get to know the poem 👥 👥

Show the children the holiday postcard or brochure again, and remind them of the poem. Ask them what they remember about it. Retell the poem using the **Storyteller** video on **Connect**, or by displaying the poem and reading it aloud to the class. Then retell the poem again, asking the children to join you in saying the last word of each verse (this rhymes with the last word of the second line of that verse).

After the retelling, choose focus activities to explore the poem in more depth.

'Structure focus' activities

More holiday 'memories' 👥 👥

- Suggest to the children that they could add more fun holiday 'memories' to the poem.
- Model an example and write it out (for example, 'I danced on top of a windmill').
- Encourage the children to make more suggestions, and to be as imaginative as possible.
- Write down the suggestions, using four trip ideas for each new verse, one per line (they needn't rhyme).
- Once all the suggestions have been noted down, read through the new verses of the poem and praise the children for their ideas.

What did I do? 👥 👥

- Display the interactive activity 'What Did I Do?'.
- Read out the first line, pausing at the missing final word.
- Ask the children if they can remember what the last word is.
- Click on the space to show three possible answers, and read them out. Praise the children if they remembered correctly.
- If they find it hard to remember, focus on the three examples as a clue.
- Repeat these steps for each line.

'Vocabulary focus' activity

Holiday photo labels 👥 👥

- Display the interactive activity 'Holiday Photo Labels' and explain that the holiday photos have lost their labels.
- Point to an image and ask the children what it shows.
- Ask the children help you find the matching label by going through each label and sounding out its first letters.
- Ask a child to come and drag the correct label to the image.
- Once all the labels are matched, encourage the children to help you to read out the words, noting any familiar sounds.

'Phonics focus' activity

'oo' and 'or' suitcase sounds 👥 👥

- Stick labels saying 'oo' and 'or' to two small suitcases (or cardboard boxes decorated to look like suitcases).
- Make a set of word cards showing words that contain 'oo' and 'or' (for example, 'soon', 'fool', 'moon', 'loop', 'fork', 'cord', 'lord' and 'horn').
- Ask the children to sound out the letters on each suitcase.
- Display the cards face down and ask children to take turns selecting one at a time.
- Ask them to sound out the word and decide which suitcase should get it.
- Stick the word onto the front of the correct suitcase.
- Repeat these steps for all cards.

EXPLORING THE POEM

PHASE 3: Performing the poem

Session 4: Let's put on a performance 👥 👥 👥 👤

Over the week, encourage the children to explore the ideas in the poem through role-play. For example:

- Ask pairs or individuals to mime one thing that they love doing during their summer holidays (for example, swimming, building sandcastles, going to a theme park ride or visiting someone).
- Ask different children to volunteer to show their mime for others, and ask the others to guess what they are doing.
- Allocate the poem's different activities to different groups, and ask them to image the holiday setting where their action happened. What else could happen on this extraordinary holiday?

During the final session, remind the children of their work so far. Show the poem again using the **Storyteller** video on **Connect**, or retell it with the children from the whiteboard. Then ask the children to work together to create a performance of the poem.

- Allocate the verses of the poem to different groups.
- Ask each group to prepare a series of mimes to act out all of the actions in their verse. They could either all mime all of the actions, or split the actions between different members of the group. Assist those with the less concrete actions (for example, riding a moonbeam) as necessary.
- Ask the groups to stand in order, and then – as you read out the poem – to give their performances at the appropriate time.
- Encourage the children to say the rhyming words at the ends of their lines with you. Ask them all to join in loudly with 'THE END'.
- If possible, film the performance for the children to watch and enjoy.

Differentiation: More confident readers may wish to read their lines along with their performances or assist you in reading out the poem.

LITERACY ACTIVITIES

Reading

Holiday sentences

- Cut out the sentences from Resource Sheet 18.1.
- Mix up each set of sentences and lay them out in front of the children.
- Explain that each sentence is about a holiday event that happened on a certain day of the week.
- Say the days of the week with the children, emphasising the initial-letter sounds.
- Read out the sentence for Monday and emphasise the initial/m/sound.
- Ask the children to read out the sentence with you. Praise their sounding and blending skills.
- Ask the children to find a sentence with a word that has the initial/t/sound for Tuesday, and then to read the sentence out, as before.
- Repeat these steps until all the days of the week are in the correct order.
- Read the sentences in order as a class.

Holiday transport

- Ask mixed-ability pairs to work on the interactive activity 'Holiday Transport', following the lines to find the label for each mode of transport.
- When each label is identified, ask the children to sound out and blend it.

Differentiation: More confident readers could start by reading the words, and follow the lines to the images.

Writing

Postcard sentences

- Model an example sentence of what you like to do on holiday (for example, 'On my holidays, I like to visit my grandmother' or 'On my holidays, I like to swim in the sea').
- Ask the children what they like to do when they are on holiday, encouraging them to choose one activity and to compose a simple oral sentence to describe it.
- Hand out copies of Resource Sheet 18.2 and model adding your sentence to your copy. Then add the name of a friend to whom the postcard could be sent, and your own name at the bottom.
- Ask the children to do the same, writing their own sentences onto their postcards.
- Then ask them to draw on the backs of their postcards to illustrate what they wrote.

Differentiation: Less confident writers may need part of the sentence written for them first, with space for them to write in select words. Encourage more confident writers to attempt more than one sentence.

Writing labels

- Ask mixed-ability pairs to work on the interactive activity 'Label Writing', arranging the letters to label the characters' bags.

Differentiation: Encourage less confident writers to look closely at the characters and to sound out the words first.

Phonics Work

Finding 'ear' words

- Ask mixed-ability pairs to work on the interactive activity 'Finding 'ear' Words', identifying the words that contain 'ear'.
- Once they have completed the task, ask the children to sound out and blend the 'ear' words.

Differentiation: Ask more confident children if they can think of any other 'ear' words.

Rucksack words

- Make a set of word cards showing words containing the letters 'ck' (for example, 'duck', 'truck', 'neck', 'black' and 'stick' – ensure you can find classroom objects or craft materials to represent each word).
- Put objects representing each word into a rucksack.
- Write out the word 'rucksack', and sound out and blend the letters into the word.
- Underline the two instances of 'ck'. Ask the children what sound the two letters make:/k/.
- Lay out the word cards and ask the children sound out and blend each one.
- Ask them to take turns removing an object from the rucksack and to match it with the correct word.

Differentiation: More confident children could repeat the activity using the 'ch', 'sh' and/or 'ng' digraphs.

CROSS-CURRICULAR ACTIVITIES

Adult-led activities 👥

My holiday scrapbook (Expressive Arts; PSHE)

- Give the children a scrapbook each before the start of the school holidays, and ask them to record their holiday experiences.
- Encourage them to decorate the front covers, and to write their names on them.
- Ask them to bring their scrapbooks in after the holidays, to show and share.

Holiday pictures (Expressive Arts; Communication and Language)

- Read through the poem again.
- Ask the children to discuss which holiday 'memory' was their favourite, and why.
- Ask them to draw how they see the memory, using coloured pencils or pens.
- Write the verse line under each picture, and display them in verse order.

Differentiation: Ask fast finishers also to draw any memories that have not been covered, to complete the poem.

Model transport (Expressive Arts; Understanding the World)

- Look at different types of transport that are used for holiday travel (for example, aeroplanes, buses, ferries and cars).
- Ask the children to make models of the different types of transport using various craft materials. Encourage them to make at least one large cardboard model that could be painted by a group and then used for imaginary play.

Child-led activities 👥 👥 👤

Packing my case (Communication and Language; Understanding the World)

- Ask talk partners or small groups to discuss what they might need if they went on holiday.
- They could consider different kinds of holidays, before choosing one for which to plan.
- When they have chosen a holiday, they should make a list (of pictures or words) of what they would need or like to take with them.

Tickets and passengers (Communication and Language; PSHE)

- Set up a ticket office and play money, and encourage the children to take turns being ticket sellers and passengers.
- Then encourage them to role-pay travelling to their holiday, using any large model transport they have created (see 'Model transport' activity above).

Different settings (Communication and Language; Understanding the World)

- Set up different world settings in different sections of the classroom, using images and/or props.
- Ask the children to role-play being on holiday there. Ask them what fantastic activities will they do.

Picture montage (PSHE; Communication and Language)

- Ask the children to bring in images of trips they have enjoyed, and display them as a montage.
- Ask the children to look at and discuss the images with their friends.

SEQUENCE ASSESSMENT

Communication and Language

- Does the child join in with and recognise repeated refrains and anticipate the end phrase in a poem?
- Has the child extended their vocabulary by exploring the meanings and sounds of new words?
- Does the child use talk to organise, sequence and clarify thinking and ideas about the poem?
- Does the child use language to imagine and recreate roles and experiences in play situations?

Reading

- Can the child recognise rhythm in the poem's verses?
- Can the child anticipate key words and rhymes in the poem?
- Can the child hear initial sounds for words?
- Can the child segment and blend sounds in words?
- Can the child recognise the sounds for the graphemes 'oo', 'or, 'ear' and 'ck'?
- Can the child read simple sentences?

Writing

- Can the child segment and blend sounds in words?
- Can the child use some clearly identifiable letters to communicate meaning, representing some sounds correctly and in sequence?
- Can the child begin to write labels and words for captions?
- Can the child write simple sentences?

Review of the Big Picture

At the end of this sequence, discuss with the children what they liked about the poem. Ask: *Why were the trips not everyday experiences? Which trips did you like most, and why? What rhyming words can you remember?*

Encourage each child to show and explain examples of their writing and reading achievements, and any cross-curricular activities they enjoyed.

Use the 'Pupil observation chart' to record each child's responses and attainment.

Body Parts

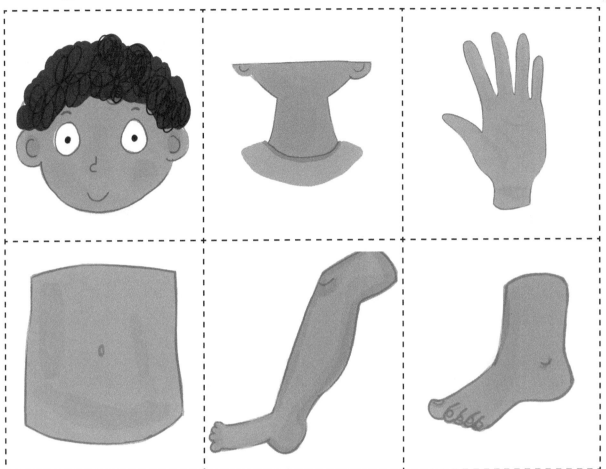

head	**n**eck	**h**and
tummy	**l**eg	**f**oot

Split-pin Puppet

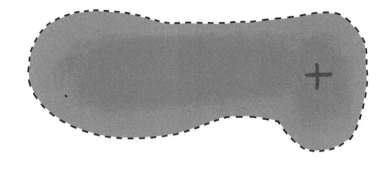

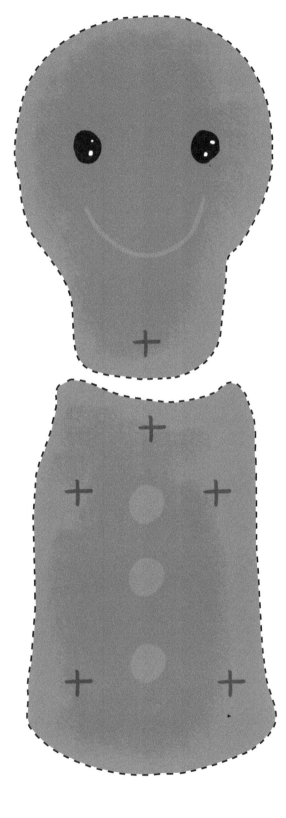

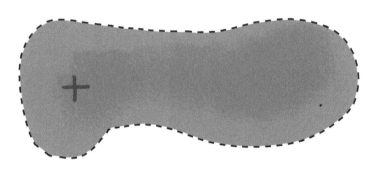

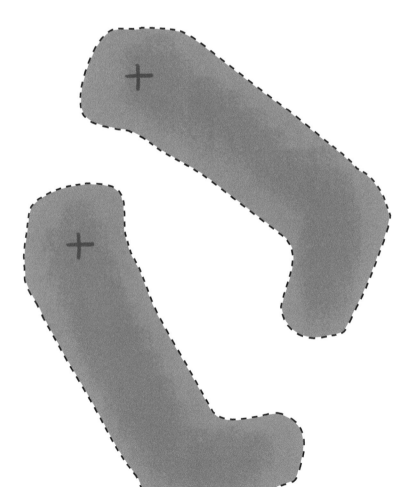

Rhyming Words (Part A)

dance
naughty
song
clay
joke
rhyme

Rhyming Words (Part B)

France
forty
long
stay
cloak
time

Bunny Toy Template

stitch before stuffing

leave open for stuffing

My Favourite Colour

_____

is my favourite colour;

I'm painting like the

_____ ,

_____ ,

and

_____ .

x, qu and zz Cards

fix	box	Max
quick	quack	quid
buzz	fizz	jazz

Elmer's Rainbow Hunt

Rainbow Word Board

r

o

y

g

b

p

Rainbow Word Cards

red	rug	ram	rib
off	on	ox	odd
yam	yes	yet	yak
got	gum	get	gap
bat	bun	bog	bit
pot	pan	peg	pip

Rangoli Patterns

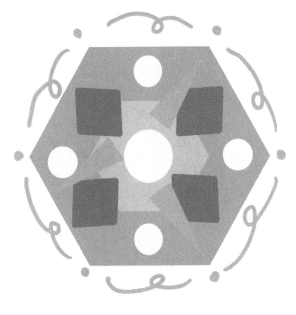

Rama and Sita Story Map

Rama and Sita Story Map

How Apples Grow

'The Enormous Potato' Storyboard

Who Pulled the Potato?

king	**c**at	**d**og	**s**nail
farmer	**p**arrot	**J**ack	**J**ill
clown	**c**ow	**g**oat	**s**heep
cook	**d**uck	**q**ueen	**p**otato

Beanstalk Sentences

Tom got a cup.

Tom put the wet wool in the cup.

Tom put a bean in the cup.

Tom put his cup in the sun.

The bean had a stem.

The stem got big.

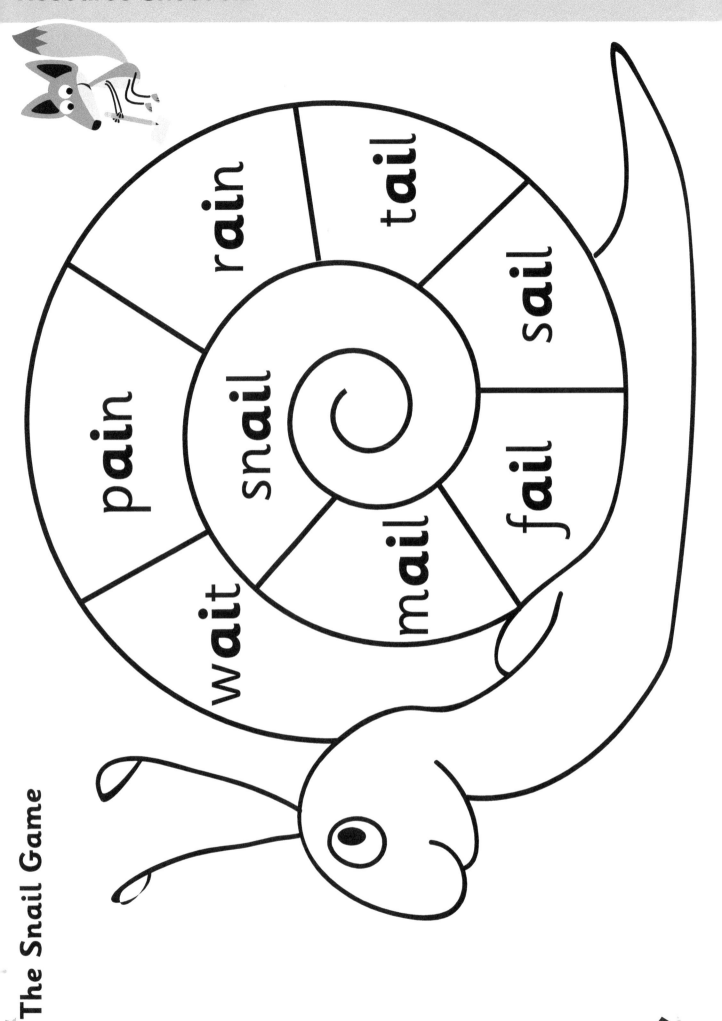

The Snail Game

Story Puppets

Sequencing 'Henny Penny'

Bee Finger Puppets

Honeycomb Templates

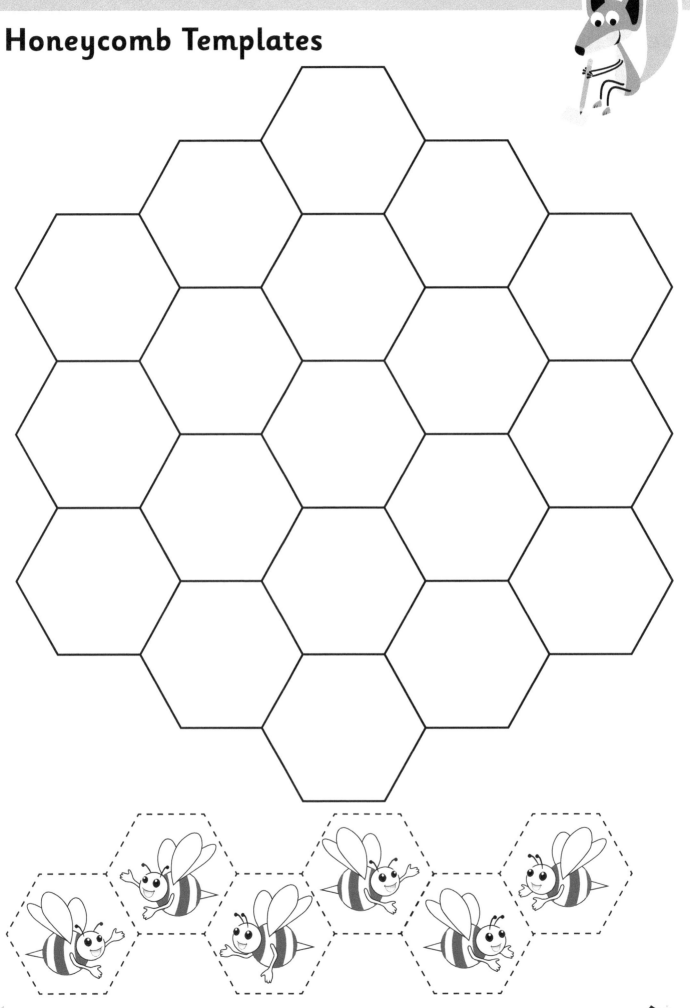

Bee Rhymes

What Do You Suppose

Poem lines	Suggested actions
What do you suppose?	Watch finger as it flies through
A bee sat on my nose.	the air and lands on your nose
Then what do you think?	
He gave me a wink.	Wink
He said, "I beg your pardon,	
I thought you were a garden."	Shrug and smile

Five Busy Bees

Poem lines	Suggested actions
Five busy bees on a lovely spring day.	Hold up five fingers
This one said, "Let's fly away."	Wiggle thumb
This one said "We'll drink some nectar sweet."	Wiggle first finger
This one said, "Let's get pollen on our feet."	Wiggle second finger
This one said "And then we'll make some honey."	Wiggle third finger
This one said "Good thing it's warm and sunny."	Wiggle little finger
So the five busy bees went flying along	Fly hand around, wiggling fingers
Singing a happy honeybee song.	
Bzzzzzzzzzz!	Fly hand behind back

Bees

Poem lines	Suggested actions
Here is the beehive. Where are the bees?	Hold up fist
Hidden away, where nobody sees.	Move other hand around fist
Watch and you'll see them come out of the hive:	Bend head close to fist
One, two, three, four, five!	Hold up fingers up one at a time
Bzzzzzzzz... all fly away!	Wave fingers; fly hand behind back

Rock-pool Creatures

Word Shells

Tentacle 'th' Words

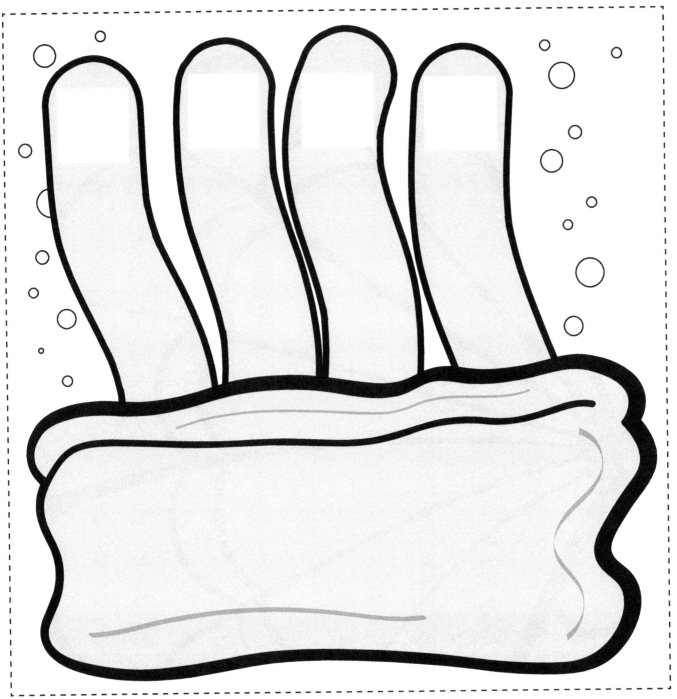

th	i	n	w
p	e	m	s
b	a	t	ck

Resource Sheet 13.1

Hot or Cold?

'k' Words

Kite Template

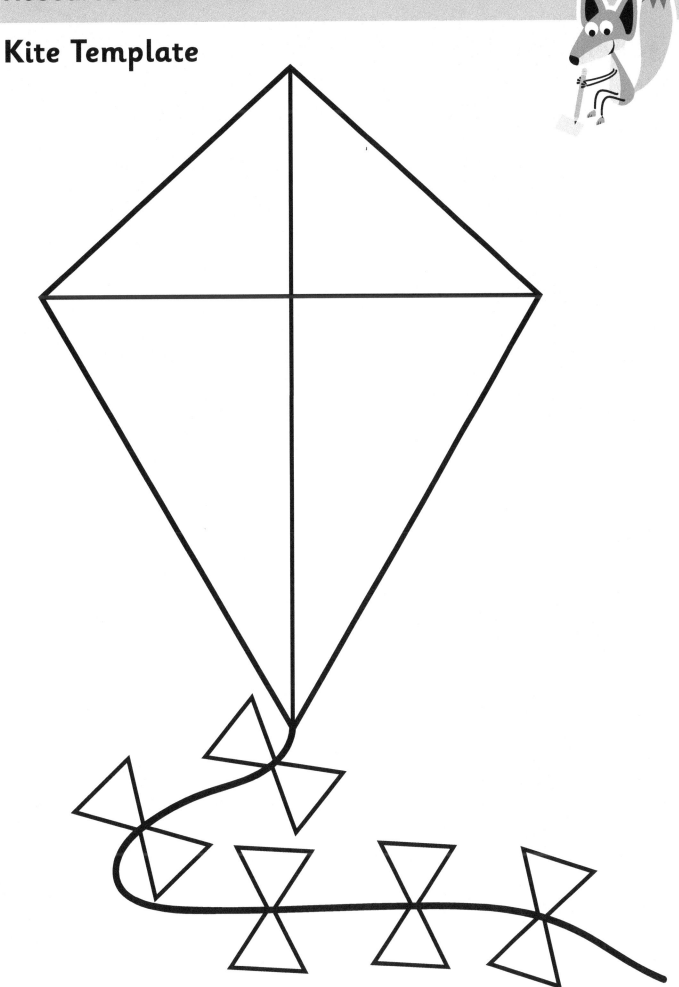

Sequencing 'The Magic Bed'

Georgie gets a magic bed.

Georgie reads to gnomes and fairies.

Georgie helps the lost tiger.

Georgie finds a treasure chest.

Georgie swims with dolphins.

Georgie helps the tired geese.

Georgie has a race with witches.

Georgie goes on holiday.

Georgie saves his bed from the dump.

Georgie goes on another magic trip.

Magic Objects

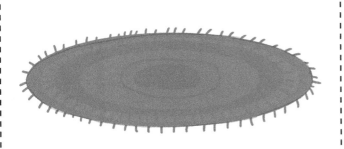

My Magic Object

This is my magic

_____ .

The Boy's Day

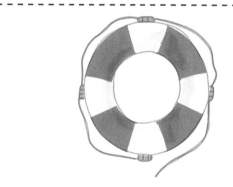

Space Labels

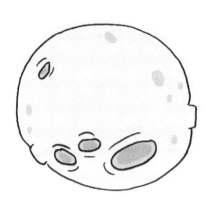
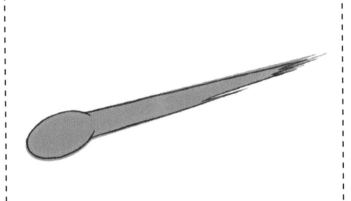
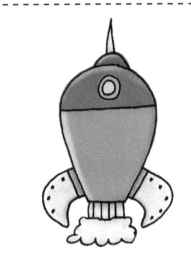

sun	comet	star
moon	rocket	planet

Carnival Float Card

My Carnival

This is the __teel __and.

This is a __loat.

This is a __iger costume.

This is a __ing.

This is a __ragon.

Kiswahili Words

Mama .... Mother
'Ma-ma'

Mzee .... Alderman
'Mm-**zay**'

Bibi .... Ms
'Bee-bee'

Bwana .... Mr
'Buh-**wah**-na'

Rafiki .... Friend
'Rah-**fee**-kee'

Habari za asubuhi? .... What's new this morning?
'Ha-**bar**-ee zah ah-suh-**boo**-ee'

Hodi! .... Here I am!
'Hoe-dee'

Karibu .... Welcome
'Kah-**ree**-boo'

Jambo! .... Hello!
'Jam-bo'

Asante sana .... Thank you
'Uh-**sahn**-tay **sahn**-ah'

Story Object Labels

hut	**c**hicken
fish	**b**ag

cows	**c**oin	**p**ot
trees	**p**epper	**l**izard

Mama Panya's Pancakes

Makes around 6 pancakes

Ingredients:

- 150 g plain flour
- 500 ml cold water
- 5 tbsp vegetable oil
- $\frac{1}{2}$ tsp salt
- $\frac{1}{2}$ tsp ground cardamom (or nutmeg)
- $\frac{1}{2}$ tsp cayenne pepper or ground chilli flakes

Equipment:

- Weighing scales
- Measuring jug
- Tbsp and tsp measures
- Mixing bowl
- Wooden spoon
- Non-stick frying pan
- Hob
- Ladle
- Spatula

Method:

1. Mix all the ingredients together to form a lumpy batter.
2. Put a non-stick frying pan on medium-low heat.
3. Put a ladle of batter into the frying pan, and tilt the pan to spread the batter.
4. When small bubbles start to appear, flip the pancake.
5. When the pancake begins to lift from the pan, it is ready.

Holiday Sentences

On **M**onday, I had a chat with a zebra.

On **T**uesday, I met a robot.

On **W**ednesday, I swam with a fish.

On **Th**ursday, I had tea with the Queen.

On **F**riday, I played football with a snail.

On **S**aturday, I dug up a chest of coins.

On **S**unday, I ran up and down a high hill.

My Holiday Postcard

Dear

On my holiday, I like

From

Workbook Answers

The alphabet

1. [Assessed orally]
2. [Assessed orally]
3. Ana, Sam, Tim

Initial letters 1

1. h–hat, n–nut, m–mat, s–sun, a–ant, p–pan, t–tap
2. cat
3. leg, log; pen, peg; tin, top; map, mud
4. hat, mug, bag

Initial letters 2

1. [Assessed orally]
2. pan, bed, net, fox, rug
3. 'v' column: van; 'w' column: wet; 'j' column: jam

Reading and writing names

1. Bella, Tom
2. [The child should draw their favourite character.]
   [The child should write the name of the character drawn and their own name, using upper-case initial letters.]
3. [The child should circle the books and computer.]

Reading and writing words

1. shed, bed, duck
2. fox, shell

CVCC words

1. tent: sent, bent, dent; band: hand, sand, land
2. nest, wind

CCVC words

1. frog, drum, plug, crab
2. trip–skip, clap–trap, trot–spot, slug–plug
3. pram, step, twig, drop, slug
4. plum, drum, flap, clap

Tricky and regular words

1. [Assessed orally; the child should also link matching words on the grid]
2. [Children's responses will vary, depending on what they find tricky or easy to learn. The most common responses may be:] to, the, go, she, my
3. [Children's responses will vary, depending on what they find tricky or easy to learn. The most common responses may be:] no, the, go, I, she
4. no, he, go, the, was, by

Words containing 'ff', 'll', 'ss', 'zz', 'ck' and 'qu'

1. cliff, huff, hill, well, mess, toss, whizz, buzz
2. sock, kick, pack, neck, pick, duck
3. queen, quite, quill, quick
4. bell, cliff, buzz, dress, duck, queen [Child's sentences assessed orally]

Words containing 'ch', 'sh', 'th' and 'ng'

1. teacher, push, moth
2. shell, chick, ring, bath

Words containing 'ai', 'ee' and 'igh'

1. train; tail, nail, sail, chain, rain
2. jeep, train, light

Words containing 'oo' and 'oa'

1. moon; boot, pool, spoon, loop, hoop
2. boat, food, goat, roof

Words containing 'or' and 'ar'

1. fork; stork, form, sort, torn
2. cart; harp, farm, barn, star, part

Words containing 'ur' and 'ow'

1. turnip; burn, hurt, fur, turn, curl
2. clown, cow
3. turkey, town, crown, purse

Words containing 'oi'

1. coin; coil, join, boil, spoil
2. noise, voice
3. coins, foil, soil

Words containing 'air'

1. chair; hair, air, pair, fair
2. [In any order:] fair, chair, pair, hair

Words containing 'ear' and 'er'

1. near, hear, year, tear, fear, dear
2. farmer, singer, jumper, summer

Reading and writing sentences

1. [The child should link each sentence with the matching image.]
2. The cat is in the tree.
3. a. 4, b. 5
4. Fred had a jam bun.
5. [The child should write one complete sentence describing any aspect(s) of the image.]